It's All a Lie

Revisiting the History of Government's abuse of Power and Money

A Handbook for Citizens of the World

By Robert W. Delaplain

Cover Design:

Symbolic Fist of Socialism – attributed to
Vecteezy.com

Image of Skulls of Khmer Rouge Victims
Page URL:
https://commons.wikimedia.org/wiki/File:Skulls_of_th
e_victims_of_the_Khmer_Rouge_occupation_of_Cam
bodia.jpg
Attribution:
istolethetv from Hong Kong, China, CC BY 2.0
<https://creativecommons.org/licenses/by/2.0>, via
Wikimedia Commons

Contents

DEDICATION

TO MY CHILDREN DAVID AND LISA WHO ARE
IN SEARCH OF TRUTH.

For those, after reading the following chapters, who remain unconvinced *It's All a Lie*, I only ask that you take the time to visit your local politicians and ask them one question: "What are you doing with my tax money?"

Question their response!

Introduction

"All truth passes through three stages. First, it is ridiculed. Second, it is violently opposed. Third, it is accepted as being self-evident." ~**Arthur Schopenhauer**

Why am I writing this story? I started my journey when I was young as a product of the U.S. educational system and ultimately graduating from an Ivy League University. I believed that I had the tools needed for life and an understanding the world. However, I have realized that much of what I was taught was not true.

My understanding and foundation of thought has been rebuilt as I have learned many lessons on my journey. These lessons are difficult to explain over a dinner conversation and when making the effort to clarify a situation, the discussion is often interrupted or there is not enough time to have a healthy conversation. As time went on, I felt that we truly needed a good overall coverage of the lies that we are being told as well as some historical perspective to better explain why the lies are needed in the first place. These lessons are difficult to communicate and explain without the right information and background. I felt compelled to share my perspective.

I've been fortunate to have the opportunity to travel the world throughout my career, living and working overseas in third world countries for over sixteen years. It was an opportunity to learn the local cultures and languages. I originally came from the school of thought that the U.S. system of capitalism and governmental rule through our U.S. Constitution is the best system, and these third world countries are backwards. Most Americans who do not travel outside of the US often carry this arrogant perspective. However, on my journeys through North and South America and Asia I learned that within these countries, even the poorest citizens survive, thrive, are happier and find solutions despite their governments failing them. People are not homeless, nor are they suffering from drug addiction or depression. It struck me as to how could this be possible? We are supposed to be the greatest nation on earth.

Why are some countries wealthy and others poor? What makes the difference? In Venezuela, millions of people are fleeing the country, walking out into Brazil and Colombia. Why does this happen? What are the differences between governments? Many of these countries declare themselves to be democracies. I was astounded by the fact that during presidential elections over 90% of the population votes in many of these third world nations. If they are democracies, why are they impoverished? In all cases, when studying the economies and history, it can be concluded that the wealth of the nation is defined by the amount of government, not the type. The more limited and smaller the government institutions, the more it leaves opportunity for wealth and prosperity creation through free market capitalism. As governments grow with larger bureaucracies, increasing taxes and creating debt to fund their programs, the poorer the nation.

The connection between an impoverished nation and a democracy is that politicians need your votes. They buy them through promoting social welfare programs of which its poor citizens support during elections. Simply put, they buy votes with handouts using the democratic system. These programs, when implemented, are poorly managed and never executed as needed for society, further impoverishing the people.

My favorite story from Venezuela is after the high inflation from the government printing too much money to fund its socialist programs, they began to implement price controls on industries. One of the first items impacted was the toilet paper supply. As price controls went into effect, toilet paper shortages arose. The people became angry. Nicolas Maduro's government made a speech to the people explaining to them that the problem of the toilet paper shortages is because the Venezuelan people are eating too well and therefore using too much toilet paper. It is hard to imagine how such a lie could even be uttered when you understood how much the people were suffering.

Through my journeys, I've experienced many similar stories from these countries. There is a common theme: corrupt government leaders, robbing the coffers of wealth from the nation for themselves leaving the nation's people indebted and impoverished. The politicians all struggle in vain to maintain their power. Election fraud runs rampant. They also know that by buying the votes of people with social welfare programs, their chances of reelection improves. Everything they tell the people is a lie.

As a nation descends into poverty, the disparity between the rich and poor increases. The middle class is hollowed out, and the majority of the population is left impoverished. The politicians seize on this opportunity to further expand their programs knowing that the rich are few in number and don't have enough votes to stop them in a democratic election. The masses of poor support the politicians in elections that are handing out ever more socialism. This cycle continues over and over until the nation enters hyperinflation through currency destruction as happened in Venezuela. The peoples only choice is to "vote with their feet," walking out of their homeland to another country if they want to avoid starvation.

"It's not who votes that counts, it's who counts the votes."

What do you expect from Third World Banana Republics run by tin-pot dictatorships? I would think America has a better system. We don't have this problem in the good ol' USA, or do we? I began to look closely at our own country, studying our history. I realized that our situation as Americans is no different. Our history reveals a narrative from our government fraught with lies not much different than Venezuela's. We are no longer the nation our Founding Fathers built.

This is not a story to argue politics from a conservative versus liberal perspective. The information and ideas shared in my story are intended to promote healthy discussion and debate amongst ourselves to better understand the reality of our situation today. Armed with better information on how we arrived at this point in history, we may make better decisions going forward.

When reading the chapters ahead, if you find yourself in disbelief, feel free to dig into more research and learn more about the subjects. The question to ask yourself is which narrative is working to protect power and control? With today's internet capability, researching these topics is very easy and I will leave you with many recommended books and web site links with QR codes. *(Simply slide your mobile phone's camera over the code, let it focus and click on the link that appears. You will go directly to the website.)* For each of these chapters ahead, many great books have been written with details and specifics which I also invite you to read.

When reading the chapters ahead, feel free to skip around to those chapters of most interest. I hope that you enjoy learning about our reality as much as I have!

Democracy

The Thinker
Billy Hathorn at English Wikipedia, CC BY-SA 3.0
<https://creativecommons.org/licenses/by-sa/3.0>, via Wikimedia Commons
Democracy

"Democracy is two wolves and a lamb voting on what to have for lunch. Liberty is a well-armed lamb contesting the vote." **~Benjamin Franklin**

Listening to a politician espouse the virtues of spreading democracy in foreign countries often leads us to believe that we as Americans offer the right solution. We have a better government than they have. We often hear our politicians use the word democracy in a way which seemingly elevates our government system over others. We are left to believe that these countries are primitive and corrupt, which implies that ours is advanced and honorable.

Democracy is an easy word to use in a slogan to rally its people to support a cause in a foreign country. We believe that we are righteous, and they need us. Democracy justifies our purpose for foreign aid, wars, and intervention.

Constitution_Pg1of4_AC.jpg: Constitutional Convention derivative work: Bluszczokrzew, Public domain, via Wikimedia Commons

"Mankind will in time discover that unbridled majorities are as tyrannical and cruel as unlimited despots." ~**John Adams**

The truth is we are not a democracy. The word "Democracy" does not even exist in our Constitution, National Anthem, nor in the Pledge of Allegiance. The Founding Fathers understood the dangers of a democracy. They knew history well and understood how all democracies failed in a "violent death" as James Madison stated. He explained in the Federalist Papers why a democracy is a poor choice of government. It is an institution giving power to the majority to oppress the minority. Simply put "Mob Rule."

As an example, freedom of religion was a priority to the States signing the Constitution, therefore Thomas Jefferson included clearly in the 1st Amendment this right. Many people just left Europe where their religion was persecuted. Freedom of religion was the core to the new countries beliefs and to ratify the Constitution they needed to be assured that they were not signing up for another monarchy or oppressive government. Let us think about how freedom of religion would work in a democracy? It would fail immediately, as those representing the majority religion would quickly begin to make it difficult for minority religions.

The importance of our Republic is remembered in the anecdote from when those waiting outside the Constitutional Convention asked Benjamin Franklin "What government have you given us?" and he replied, "A Republic, if you can keep it."

"Hence it is that such democracies have ever been spectacles of turbulence and contention; have ever been found incompatible with personal security or the rights of property; and have in general been as short in their lives as they have been violent in their death." **~James Madison, Federalist Paper 10**

Why do politicians continue to use the word democracy? Why are we all taught this lie from grade school? Those with the power want us to believe that we have a say in our government. They want us to understand that we are not a monarch. It is a simple idea to teach and accept. We feel empowered as we vote. We are part of the process; however, it also teaches us to accept the situation when our ideas are different from the ruling majority. We say to ourselves, "Oh well, we are not in power, let's hope for the next election." We end up as a society that is oppressed with only a hope for a future that is better. This is not what our Founding

Fathers had in mind. They carefully wrote our Constitution as a Republic to prevent this mob rule form of government. They understood a democracy ends protecting the majority, but a Republic such as our Constitution protects the minority.

"An elective despotism was not the government we fought for" ~**Thomas Jefferson, Notes on Virginia Q.XIII, 1782.**

A Republic is a more complex conversation for a teacher to have with a student. Our Constitution is written to carefully limit the power of the Federal Government and a Republic is designed to make it very difficult for a majority "mob rule." The public-school system, which is "The Government", is at odds with itself if to explain the dangers of government. It would be like the king of his country explaining how to weaken his own power. No king wants to give up his power. Therefore, our education system from K-12 and the Universities all have a deep motivation to lie about our form of government. Through decades of educating the masses and omitting the critical features of our Republic, we develop as a society that ultimately ignores the Constitution and the principles that our Founding Fathers instituted. We have become a society believing that we are a democracy. This is a great lie.

The Constitution of the United States of America

Signing of the Constitution of the United States
Howard Chandler Christy, Public domain, via Wikimedia Commons

"The pillars of our prosperity are the most thriving when left most free to individual enterprise." **~Thomas Jefferson**

We should start with a brief aside explaining several of the important features of our Constitution, which by design, limits the power of the federal government and prevents a situation where a majority ruling may oppress a minority group. Our Constitution is a document that is very clearly written. You do not need a law degree to understand its meaning. Anyone with an 8th grade education can read it and understand how it should be applied to govern our country.

Our Founding Fathers created the first system of government in the history of the world with the intention to severely limit the power of a Federal Government. As stated in the 10th Amendment, all other power belongs to States and individuals. After the Constitution was written, the Founding Fathers worked to convince the states to ratify the document. They knew there was a great fear of signing on to another oppressive form of government. Therefore, they wrote many follow-up documents further explaining the meaning and intention for such a structure. These writings are captured in the Federalist Papers. The author of the Constitution, James Madison, wrote several documents in the Federalist Papers.

From the time our country was founded to the start of WWI in 1914, our country prospered at a rate never realized in human history. A truly free market capitalist economy, innovation and investment in start-up enterprises ran unhindered by bureaucracy and regulations. The transformation from an almost completely agrarian society into the industrial revolution, lifted 80% of the population out of poverty. Economic freedom existed to a degree that allowed entrepreneurs and businessmen to work together to bring solutions and products to markets all in search for profit, the core driver of free market capitalism. Electricity, medicines, phones, radio, cars, trains, planes, and ships all developed at an astounding pace. Foreigners from all over the world would travel to visit the U.S. in the late 1800's and early 1900's to marvel at our growth and prosperity. This transformation was a rare example in world history where government was limited and held in check by an incredibly well written document structured to give the power to the individuals.

"Those who would give up essential liberty, to purchase a little temporary safety, deserve neither liberty nor safety." **~Benjamin Franklin**

Highlights of our Republic,

1. Three branches of government providing a system of "checks and balances" to avoid any one single branch from becoming too powerful and overstepping its authority.

2. Article I: Congress simply creates the laws needed for the nation.

However, the reach of these laws is with the understanding that they apply only to the powers authorized in Article I Section 8,

> *"The Congress shall have Power To*
>
> *lay and collect Taxes, Duties, Imposts and Excises, to pay the Debts and provide for the common Defense and general Welfare of the United States; but all Duties, Imposts and Excises shall be uniform throughout the United States;*
> *To borrow Money on the credit of the United States;*
> *To regulate Commerce with foreign Nations, and among the several States, and with the Indian Tribes;*
> *To establish a uniform Rule of Naturalization, and uniform Laws about Bankruptcies throughout the United States;*
> *To coin Money, regulate the Value thereof, and of foreign Coin, and fix the Standard of Weights and Measures;*

To provide for the Punishment of counterfeiting the Securities and current Coin of the United States;

To establish Post Offices and post Roads;

To promote the Progress of Science and useful Arts, by securing for limited Times to Authors and Inventors the exclusive Right to their respective Writings and Discoveries;

To constitute Tribunals inferior to the supreme Court;

To define and punish Piracies and Felonies committed on the high Seas, and Offenses against the Law of Nations;

To declare War, grant Letters of Marque and Reprisal, and make Rules concerning Captures on Land and Water;

To raise and support Armies, but no Appropriation of Money to that Use shall be for a longer Term than two Years;

To provide and maintain a Navy;

To make Rules for the Government and Regulation of the land and naval Forces;

To provide for calling forth the Militia to execute the Laws of the Union, suppress Insurrections and repel Invasions;

To provide for organizing, arming, and disciplining, the Militia, and for governing such Part of them as may be employed in the Service of the United States, reserving to the States respectively, the Appointment of the Officers, and the Authority of training the Militia according to the discipline prescribed by Congress;

To exercise exclusive Legislation in all Cases whatsoever, over such District (not exceeding ten Miles square) as may, by

Cession of particular States, and the Acceptance of Congress, become the Seat of the Government of the United States, and to exercise like Authority over all Places purchased by the Consent of the Legislature of the State in which the Same shall be, for the Erection of Forts, Magazines, Arsenals, dock-Yards and other needful Buildings; -And To make all Laws which shall be necessary and proper for carrying into Execution the foregoing Powers, and all other Powers vested by this Constitution in the Government of the United States, or in any Department or Officer thereof."

That's it! Our Congress can feel free to stop now! Any laws created outside of these authorized powers, are unconstitutional. The power to create laws outside of these powers lies with the States or individuals. If congress would like to create a law outside of those listed in Article I, Section 8, they must amend the Constitution. For example, we passed the 18th Amendment, the regarding prohibition of alcohol, which took effect in 1920. However, for the most part the limiting authority of Article I, Section 8 has continuously been ignored by our congress for almost the last 100 years.

It could even be argued now that many of these powers authorized were in error when understanding the power of free market capitalism. When fully understanding the logic and implications of the Founding Fathers' documents and the capability of entrepreneurs to meet society's needs the free market will often find needed solutions. As an example, the US post office should be eliminated from the responsibility of the Federal government. Federal Express, DHL and UPS, as well as digital email, have shown that our post office is a relic of the past. Inefficient and bureaucratic, it has become a tool used for sending junk mail at below cost, at the expense of the taxpayer. They hold a monopoly over mail, and if eliminated, a free-market enterprise would fill its place meeting the needs of our society. Maybe at the time, Benjamin Franklin thought it necessary, but he failed to realize that he could have started his own post office as a profitable private business. If not him, someone else would have.

3. Article II: The Executive branch signs the laws into effect, but also holds the power to veto those laws. Congress may override a veto with two-thirds approval from both houses of Congress. The Constitution did not give the President the power to make law, as that would bring us closer to a monarch.

The President does have a voice of leadership for our government and our country. This unspoken "power" leaves open the door to persuading our nation with an agenda. Herein lies a great danger to our freedoms if used inappropriately. However, on the other hand, this bully pulpit could be used to expose the lies and corruption that exists within other branches of our government, but sadly it rarely is used as such.

4. Article III: The Supreme Court holds the power to strike down a law which is not authorized in the Constitution. In doing so, the power of the law is returned to the states and/or individuals. Its only role is to uphold the Constitution, not to decide on policy or if laws are just. When we truly understand this function, we realize that most of the laws passed by our congress are unconstitutional. However, our Supreme court has ignored its responsibility for the last 100 years, allowing government programs to exist on the Federal level that are clearly not in the Constitution.

5. Bill of Rights (Amendments 1-10): These were added by Thomas Jefferson to add an additional level of security to the rights and freedoms of the citizens. They clearly state freedoms given to the individual to protect us from the oppression of government.

    The 10th Amendment becomes the most powerful in understanding the division of authority of the Federal Government from the States or individual:

    "The powers not delegated to the United States by the Constitution, nor prohibited by it to the States, are reserved to the States respectively, or to the people."

It is very clear, that our Founding Fathers understood that the power of our government needed to be limited. Our society for the first 125 years of the new

Republic understood this concept as well and they were rewarded with enormous prosperity.

This document, however, cannot be taken for granted. Keep in mind that even in China's Constitution they state:

> "Article 35. Citizens of the People's Republic of China enjoy freedom of speech, of the press, of assembly, of association, of procession, and of demonstration."

Having it written in the Constitution does not guarantee these rights. In our Constitution, it is the role of the Supreme Court to enforce the Constitution. Their responsibility is to strike down all laws and government overreach to protect the citizens from powers not delegated to the Federal government explicitly in the Constitution. Unfortunately, the Supreme has been remiss in this responsibility for almost 100 years. The people must act against unconstitutional laws and behavior of the Federal Government.

Propaganda

By the Oxford Language's definition, **propaganda** means *"information, especially of a biased or misleading nature, used to promote or publicize a particular political cause or point of view."*

By the Merriam-Webster definition, a **lie** means *"to make an untrue statement with intent to deceive."*

Note that these definitions are remarkably similar in meaning.

Fidel Castro and his men in the Sierra Maestra
Unknown author: Public domain, via Wikimedia Commons

Under socialist rule, as in Cuba or in the U.S.S.R., there is only one state news TV, print and radio source of information. This control is critical to maintaining a narrative that does not deviate from the government's position. No other source is permitted. The population is pumped with propaganda creating satisfaction and loyalty to the State without the information and facts to understand any different perspective. It would be safe to say everything told to them is a lie and the people are fed information that is not reality. Most of the population will believe this information. The one critical link for people to finding truth is exposure to alternate information. They may then evaluate which version makes more sense or is more logical.

"If you tell a lie big enough and keep repeating it, people will eventually come to believe it. The lie can be maintained only for such time as the State can shield the people from the political, economic and/or military consequences of the lie. It thus becomes vitally important for the State to use all its powers to repress dissent, for the truth is the mortal enemy of the lie, and thus by extension, the truth is the greatest enemy of the State."
~Joseph Goebbels,
Hilter's Minister of Propaganda

Lost to most citizens is the motivation of those in power and their desire to remain in power. All tyrannical governments need to have this structure of propaganda. The greatest example of its use was Hitler's Minister of Propaganda, Paul Joseph Goebbels. His use of radio and film skillfully communicated the message needed by the Nazi party. It would be correct to believe that most Americans would understand this structure to be horrific. "Freedom of press and speech is being suppressed," they would say. Americans look at this type of regime as a form of tyranny, and we would never permit that level of governmental control in our own country.

"If liberty means anything at all, it means the right to tell people what they do not want to hear."
~**George Orwell**

But let us take a closer look at our own system of news media and information. Are we as a society truly benefiting from a free press and free speech? Are we allowed to freely discuss and debate all opposing arguments? If one narrative is a lie, then opposition would be voiced. Every situation will have at least two points of view. It would be the responsibility of good journalism to reveal these to the public. If one of the arguments is not discussed, omitted, or ignored, then there is a great danger to the society of the influence of propaganda which would be pushing an agenda of a few onto a society. Even if the Constitution states freedom of press and speech, in practice this may not be the case.

"When you want to help people, you tell them the truth. When you want to help yourself, you tell them what they want to hear." ~**Thomas Sowell**

In our modern world, mainstream media machines work tirelessly to send out an agenda. Just watch CNN for ten minutes and you will realize the message they are promoting. But is this agenda propaganda? What makes it any different from the news fed to the people of Cuba? It is amazing to observe on a Sunday morning all the mainstream media talk shows discuss the same narrative, using the same words and talking points. The messaging to the public is eerily like a socialist dictatorship.

Where are the opposing views? There are none. CNN, MSN, NBC, ABC, NPR, PBS, Boston Globe, Washington Post, and the New York Times all carry the same message daily. How is it possible that no dissenting point of view is discussed in depth? This is no coincidence. It is by design, and what is astonishing is the correlation between their message and the message you would expect from a powerful government working to keep the population satisfied, such as in Cuba today.

"Control the media and you control the minds of the people." ~**Joseph Stalin**

This wasn't always the situation in the US. In 1800s, when laws were being passed in Congress, there was deep debate amongst the population. Newspaper editors and politicians discussed strong arguments which rooted out the true meaning of our principles and freedoms.

What we do have today is an internet tool in which to research and make available information and discussion that doesn't agree with the mainstream news. However, most people do not have the time, nor the desire to search for this information. The effort seems daunting. People are afraid to read opposing arguments and learn new positions. Many believe that these sources may not be credible. The government preys on this weakness further, creating the "Trusted News Initiative" organized by the BBC to stop the spread of "misinformation." The Biden Administration creates George Orwell's "Ministry of Truth" named the Disinformation Governance Board, which they claim to combat "misinformation". Clearly the intent is to suppress and silence opposing voices.

Journalists today have become shills of the State. They have been trained in journalism school on how to control the narrative in a brilliantly polished form. Their use of "Experts" to promote their cause has become a tool to assure those listening that their message is accurate. True debate is avoided. Controversial points of view that attack the State are spun as conspiracy or omitted altogether.

"An expert is someone who doesn't want to learn anything new, because then he wouldn't be an expert." ~**President Harry Truman**

The pinnacle of mainstream news propaganda was on display after 9/11. The nation, riled up with anger and fear, was pumped with information that Saddam Hussein was evil. He was developing Weapons of Mass Destruction and we must not wait before he uses them. We are all schooled in how Europe sat idle while Hitler invaded Czechoslovakia. We are trained to think we cannot let this happen again. The expert "Colin Powell" was brought in as the big gun of propaganda to deliver the message that these Weapons of Mass Destruction do exist. All of Congress voted for the Iraq invasion without hesitation all based on a lie.

Yes, Saddam was probably not a nice guy. He was a ruthless dictator. But his crimes were nothing in comparison to the death and destruction we caused in his country by our war killing over 200,000 civilians. To this day the government of Iraq doesn't exist and remains in complete chaos. Where is the democracy they were supposed to get in replacement of Saddam?

In the chapters ahead, we will discuss the lies told to us in our history, of which the media has always been complicit in promoting. Jingoism and Yellow Journalism have become the norm. Journalists today have signed up for a Faustian bargain, selling their souls to the Devil for their careers and the hope of fame and fortune. They fail to take the responsibility of rooting out and explaining differing perspectives. They lie through omission. As we learn about their corrupt alignment with the State's narrative intended to hypnotize its citizens, we can safely say that everything they tell us from this point forward will also be a lie.

War

"The first casualty when war comes is truth."
~**Hiram Johnson**

There is no human activity more treacherous, horrific and destructive than war. Man against man, fighting to the death with the intention to conquer and subdue. In reality it is very difficult to bring man to this point of savagery. We are normally peaceful by nature and if left to our own accord, we often choose to support and give back to our society with the desire to help others.

How is it that we bring ourselves to such a mindful state of hatred wishing death on others? The mechanism for this is government propaganda. The State strikes fear into our hearts due to a situation of an imminent threat. People buy into this fear and rise up in anger ready to kill and obliterate those that pose this danger. The leaders of states have been using this method for thousands of years. Today their message of war propaganda is very organized and well thought out using all the tools of journalism and the propaganda machine.

The people of the nation become aligned and willing to commit crimes of war in the need to protect themselves as told to them by their leaders. The leaders know that the common man cannot resist such deceitful rhetoric. They will follow their leaders like sheep.

In an experiment developed to understand human obedience, the Milgram experiment, conducted at Yale University in 1962 demonstrated how the power of leadership and propaganda can drive normally peaceful people to commit horrific crimes of war.

Milgram Experiment, by Stanley Milgram, 1961

https://www.youtube.com/watch?v=fCV1I-_4GZQ

United States Civil War (1861–1865)

Battle of Gettysburg
Timothy H. O'Sullivan, Public domain, via Wikimedia Commons

Today we are led to believe from our history that the intent of the Civil War was to free the slaves. Undoubtedly slavery was a horrific institution that needed to be abolished, but most countries throughout the world gave up slavery around the same time without war. From a purely economic perspective, slavery was a terrible business model as well. For many such reasons, slavery ended all across the Americas around the same time.

What is different about the U.S.? Why are we being told the Civil War is about freeing slaves? Was there another reason for such a terrible war? Keep in mind this was a war in which over 700k U.S. citizens died. There was terrific destruction to our country and the impact was devastating to those soldiers and families who were involved.

When looking closer at our history, we learn that Abraham Lincoln freed the slaves in the Emancipation Proclamation, but his freedom only applied to the Confederate States. Slavery remained in several Northern Union States. The slaves that were in the Union States were not given their freedom until the 13th Amendment to our Constitution was ratified on December 6, 1865. The war had ended May 26, 1865.

The historian, Tom DiLorenzo, makes a strong argument in his books "*The Problem with Lincoln*" and "*Lincoln Unmasked*" that the war had nothing to do with freeing the slaves. He quotes Lincoln in a letter to the editor Horace Greeley, "My paramount objective in this struggle is to save the Union, and it is not either to save or destroy slavery." This alone indicates that the war was not fought for freedom of the slaves. If that were the case, Lincoln would have immediately freed the slaves in the Northern states as well. When reading the documents of our history it is clear that Lincoln's motive in freeing the slaves was only to create difficulty for the Confederacy. He hoped that the slaves would rise up and fight against the Confederate soldiers.

What else do we know about Lincoln and his opinion on slaves? As Tom DiLorenzo discusses further in his writings that Lincoln didn't care about this issue. As a matter of fact, when he married his wife Mary Todd, he married into a family of a wealthy slave owner. Over time he knew the situation was not favorable, but rather than free the slaves, as did Thomas Jefferson and George Washington, he resold them back into slavery. Imagine this fact of history in contradiction to the term the "Great Emancipator" being discussed in today's world. This perspective would be in direct opposition to the narrative our children are learning in schools today.

So why the rhetoric today as to why we fought the Civil War and what was the reason for such death and destruction of our country? Following the struggle for power at the time, we learned how Northern States had implemented trade tariffs that made it difficult for the Southern States to manage their cotton businesses. The South opposed these tariffs but didn't have the power to eliminate them in Congress. They were left with no recourse but to secede from the Union. The Southerners understood that joining the Union was voluntary and the States had the power to be independent as authorized in the Constitution. Lincoln would not stand for a divided nation. He therefore started the war with the South to bring them back into the Union of the United States.

A close look at the speeches, writings and actions of Lincoln leading up to and during the Civil War presents a very different understanding from the lies being taught today. Lies are told because it is paramount that our Federal Government retains its power over all the States. Any State wishing to leave the Union now fears war. From this perspective, it is clear where the tyranny exists. Nowhere in our Constitution does it say that a State cannot choose to leave the Union. As a matter of fact, when understanding the 10th Amendment, everything not clearly defined is left to the power of the States and individuals. For this reason alone, it can be argued that any State wishing to leave may do so. From this perspective, over 700k U.S. citizens needlessly died in the Civil War based on a lie.

Spanish-American War (1898)

USS Maine Wrecked in Havana Bay
Camilla Lawson, public domain, via Wikimedia Commons

When does a country decide to go to war? The Spanish-American War was initiated by an explosion that sank the U.S.S. Maine in the harbor of Havana, Cuba. 355 men died as a result and the media quickly assumed that the ship was torpedoed implying that it was attacked. American sentiment quickly believed that Spain was at fault escalating the desire for war. A month after the explosion, the U.S. Navy completed its investigation, concluding that the powder magazines came from an external explosion under the ship's hull. Americans were now ready for war.

Further investigations years later came to conclusions that the explosion originated internally to the ship. Questions should be asked, was it done intentionally? Did our President at the time, William

McKinley, who gave the orders to send the ship to Havana, do so with the intention to create a situation that would light a spark to rally the American public to support a war with Spain? There was great interest in expanding America's influence in the Caribbean and Central America. The control of the sugar market was important to U.S. businesses. We were looking to construct a canal through Panama as well. A war with Spain to gain control and power for American business interests would be of great benefit.

An American expansionist agenda alone could not be reason enough to begin a war with Spain. Americans needed to feel threatened. Here enters the brilliant journalistic craftsmanship of William Randolph Hearst, the master of yellow journalism. His newspapers sensationalized the incident of the sinking of U.S.S. Maine, blaming Spain. This new form of journalism aroused a strong emotional response from the American public. Even though it could be argued that they described the event as factual at the time, the journalists failed to question the narrative to better understand the truth. We went to war without a true understanding of the situation. As it turns out, the war was started based on a lie.

In his book *War and Empire*, Prof. Paul Atwood writes:

> *"The Spanish American War was fomented on outright lies and trumped-up accusations against the intended enemy. ... War fever in the general population never reached a critical temperature until the accidental sinking of the USS Maine was deliberately, and falsely, attributed to Spanish villainy. ... In a cryptic message ... Senator Lodge*

wrote: 'There may be an explosion any day in Cuba which would settle a great many things. We have a battleship in the harbor of Havana, and our fleet, which overmatches anything the Spanish have, is masked at the Dry Tortugas.'

Would our President put our own soldiers into harm's way to get us into a war? Were the lives of sailors and officers worth less than the value of gaining expansionist control into the Americas? Did Spain want a war? It was clear to the Spanish that they would lose a war with the U.S. and therefore they were not motivated to instigate one. Spain had been weakened by fighting unrest in many of its colonies. There was no desire for war with the U.S. as they knew it would result in a loss of much power under their colonial control. Understanding Spain's situation better and the U.S.' ambition to expand brings about serious questions that we as Americans need to ask.

Bonus Food for Thought:

Teddy Roosevelt, an active leader in the war, became a great beneficiary. He returns to the U.S. as a war hero and became Vice President under McKinley, who was later assassinated in 1901. Roosevelt then becomes the President of the U.S.

Coincidently, the assassin, Leon Czolgosz, is interviewed prior to the President's death by Emma Goldman, a known anarchist. She rejects his involvement in her organization based on how he responds her questions. Her conclusion interestingly enough, is that she believed he was working with the authorities or police. She didn't want him to be part of her anarchist movement. Later, the anarchists were blamed for his death.

As an another interesting note, after the assassination of President McKinley, Theodore Roosevelt immediately kicks off what we call the FBI department today. Did Roosevelt arrange his death using an elite group of assassins which later became the FBI?

World War I (1914–1918)

Lusitania Arriving in New York
Maritime Quest, Public domain, via Wikimedia Commons

World War I started on July 28, 1914, sparked by the assassination of Archduke Franz Ferdinand of Austria-Hungary, however America does not enter the war until April of 1917. The U.S. citizens at first were reluctant to join the war in Europe, but after the sinking of the RMS Lusitania on May 7, 1915, by a German U-boat, the people's sentiment changed. This event was controversial due to the fact this was a passenger ship killing 128 Americans and 1198 people in all. The Germans claimed that the ship was carrying ammunition supplies to support England. Was the Lusitania sending ammunition supplies to the allies with 1900 passengers and Americans on board?

The U.S. economy had been in a recession in 1913 and 1914 and businesses across the country were struggling. The supply of war materials to support the

British became an opportunity for many American businessmen. Morgan and other financial leaders were pushing for the U.S. to enter the war as they prospered from the boom in activity.

The historian Murray Rothbard captures the motives in his book, *"Wall Street, Banks, and American Foreign Policy" p17*:

"The Morgan-Progressive Party ploy deliberately ensured the election of Woodrow Wilson as a Democratic President. Wilson himself, until almost the time of running for President, was for several years on the board of the Morgan-controlled Mutual Life Insurance Company.

By early 1915, Secretary McAdoo was writing to Wilson hailing the "great prosperity" being brought by war exports to the Allies, and a prominent business writer wrote the following year that "War, for Europe, is meaning devastation and death; for America a bumper crop of new millionaires and a hectic hastening of prosperity revival."

American entry into World War I in April 1917 prevented negotiated peace between the warring powers, and drove the Allies forward into a peace of unconditional surrender and dismemberment, a peace which, as we have seen, set the stage for World War II. American entry thus cost countless lives on both sides, caused chaos and disruption throughout central and eastern Europe at war's end, and the consequent rise of Bolshevism, fascism, and Nazism to power in Europe. In this way, Woodrow Wilson's decision to enter the war may have been the single most fateful action of the twentieth century, causing untold and unending misery and destruction. But Morgan profits were expanded and assured." ~**Murray Rothbard, Wall Street, Banks, and American Foreign Policy" p17**

The American entrance into WWI was based on lies which are difficult to prove, however we do know that there was great motivation from our leaders with pressure from businessmen prospering from it. Our government has even acknowledged that passenger ships were carrying supplies of ammunition, which is a crime against civilians.

Also in 1918, a new organization of U.S. businessmen, the Council on Foreign Relations (CFR), began. Although claiming officially to be founded in 1921, the CFR started as a dinner for U.S. businessmen inviting key foreign players to speak. The CFR, led by the Morgans, were the same businessmen benefitting from the war. The CFR was then tasked by Woodrow Wilson to aid in drafting the terms of the Treaty of Versailles Peace agreement at the end of the war. The terms that economically destroyed Russia and Germany, leaving territorial issues unsettled and eventually bringing the U.S. back into WWII through the rise of Fascism, Nazism and Bolshevism, as Murry Rothbard mentions. The CFR's influence behind the scenes on U.S. foreign policy continues to this day. Today they continue to work to develop a world order to the benefit of American business interest.

World War II (1939-1945)

Pearl Harbor Attack, 7 December 1941
Naval History & Heritage Command, Public domain, via Wikimedia Commons

    The aggressive act of Japan's surprise attack on Pearl Harbor finally drummed up the public support needed for Congress to approve declaring war. Prior to this attack on our Navy, the public did not want to be involved in another war with Europe. The memories of the horrors of WWI remained on American's mind as many believed that entering WWI was a mistake altogether. Americans wanted to remain neutral in the war even after Germany invaded Poland. The war had been raging for more than two years in Europe and the Pacific prior to our involvement. Throughout that time, President Franklin D. Roosevelt's (FDR's) continuous effort to involve the U.S. other than supplying military aid to England had failed.

Questioning how we entered WWII is not a popular idea. Historians often view those who seek to better understand the truths behind FDR's motives are labeled revisionists with the intention of discrediting their arguments. When working to better understand the circumstances at the time, we learn how FDR manipulated Japan into attacking first. His communications provoked Japan. Believing the U.S. was going to attack and therefore knowing war was imminent, the Japanese decided to launch their attack first.

Several historians have well written books detailing the step-by-step efforts of FDR. The historian, Charles A. Beard, wrote several books explaining in detail FDR's foreign policy and motivation to join the war in Europe. *"American Foreign Policy in the Making, 1932-1940"* and *"President Roosevelt and the Coming of War, 1941"* were two of his writings that explain in depth the circumstances of the time. As well, the historian, Charles C. Tansill, author of *"Back Door to War: The Roosevelt Foreign Policy, 1933–1941"* brings more clarity to the situation. Later Patrick J. Buchanan in his book *"A Republic, Not an Empire"* continued to make the case that the U.S. did not need to enter WWII. He concludes that Germany and the Soviet Union would have eventually destroyed themselves leading to an end to the fighting.

FDR's actions to provoke the Japanese, leaving our Navy unguarded and unprepared for the attack, was his "back door" approach to angering the American people enough to join the fight. This strategy does not sound very different from the history of the Spanish-American War. Again, the American people are lied to and to this day remain confused on the events of history.

Vietnam

"Socialism is a wonderful idea. It is only as a reality that it has been disastrous. Among people of every race, color, and creed, all around the world, socialism has led to hunger in countries that used to have surplus food to export.... Nevertheless, for many of those who deal primarily in ideas, socialism remains an attractive idea -- in fact, seductive. Its every failure is explained away as due to the inadequacies of particular leaders." ~**Thomas Sowell**

George F. Kennan, a Council of Foreign Relations member on the policy planning staff, introduces America to the supposed dangers of the Soviet Union and the needed principle of "Containment which would guide America's approach to the cold war for the next four decades."

"Communism" is spreading around the world as we were told about the principle of the Domino Theory. "Communism" is evil and must be stopped.

Bonus Food for Thought:

The term "Communism" is often not understood correctly. Communism is a state that the Marxist's regimes told their followers they would reach in several hundred years. A state in the future in which they would all live the Utopian Dream of harmony, where we work for pleasure, share resources and live together in a community. In the meantime, there exists a government of

---

"Socialism." This is an important distinction between Communism and Socialism.

As the people believed in this future dream, those living under those socialist regimes suffered horrific conditions:

People's Republic of China: - Mao Zedong's efforts to industrialize his nation through the programs of the Great Leap Forward and the Cultural Revolution resulted in the deaths of over 50 million, most of whom died from famine and starvation.

China's One-Child policy (1980-2015), an effort to control population growth, resulted in mass murder for decades. One could argue that when studying the demographics of China today, it can be estimated that more than 200 million died. Culturally, the Chinese preference for boys combined with the forced limit to have only one child, girls were not wanted. Horrific reports of mass abortions and murder of baby girls arise during this period of time. Being that the entire society is complicit, we don't have accurate numbers. What we do know today is that there is a massive population disparity between boys and girls, giving us an indication of the magnitude of the atrocity.

Union of Soviet Socialist Republics, U.S.S.R. (1922-1991): - Joseph Stalin, through murder and starvation, killed over 15 million of his own people.

Nazi Germany (1933-1943) - Note that "Nazi" stood for the National Socialist German Workers Party. Six million Jews and an additional five million prisoners of war and others were murdered.

Cambodia (1975-1979) - Under the regime of Po Pot up to 2 million people die. Many are murders of political opposition, however, most of the deaths are from starvation as a result of his policies.

People's Republic of Cuba (1959 – current) – Over 140,000 murders of political opposition.

Socialist Republic of Vietnam (1954 – current) - Over 1.25 million persons of political opposition murdered.

Africa - There is no place on earth today where more people are oppressed and impoverished from Socialist Dictatorships than Africa. Throughout the entire continent, governments employ brutal military rule to maintain their power. In elections, the opposition is eliminated and the wealth of the nations is looted by tyrannical governments.

The Utopian dream of "Communism" asks the people to give up their sovereignty for the betterment of the State/Community. "Experts," smarter than the common people, will make decisions for them. It all sounds convincing until they realize the motives of those leaders. Never succeeding, the result of "Socialism" is death and impoverishment.

The Americans believed and feared that the spread of these Marxist ideologies would eventually come to threaten our homeland.

Vietnam was where our leaders were making the effort to stop this "Domino" effect. After the French leave, the country's government was weak and needed our support. China was supporting Ho Chi Minh coming down from the North. Our President, John F. Kennedy (JFK), at the beginning was rather reluctant to escalate the War. After his assassination, Lyndon B. Johnson (LBJ) worked to change that.

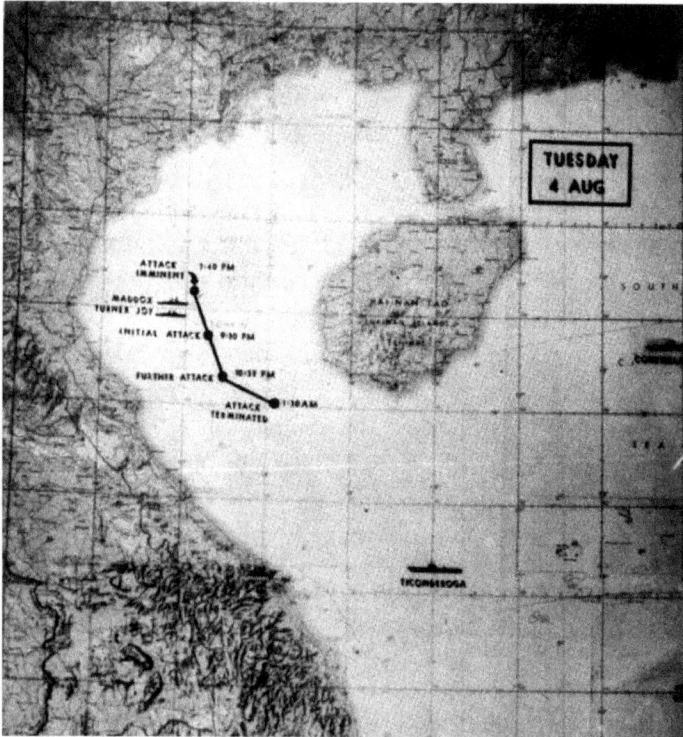

Gulf of Tonkin Incident Map of Alleged Attacks on 4 August 1964
U.S. Navy, Public domain, via Wikimedia Commons

The key turning point was what we call today the Gulf of Tonkin Incident. The Gulf of Tonkin is located off the coast of Northern Vietnam. On August 2, 1964, the U.S. Navy destroyer USS Maddox was on an intelligence gathering operation in hostile waters and was attacked by Vietnamese torpedo boats. There was no loss of life on the U.S. side and the destroyer only suffered from a bullet hole, overall, the destroyer was unscathed.

Two days later, on August 4, 1964, the Maddox was joined by another destroyer, the USS Turner Joy, in another intelligence gathering operation. The destroyers opened fire on what they believed to be an attack by Vietnamese boats from their radar information. We learn later that the 2nd attack never happened. This has been confirmed and not disputed in the narrative of our current history.

This event becomes LBJ's excuse to rally public support for escalating and ramping the U.S. into open war with the Northern Vietnamese.

LBJ makes an historic speech on August 4th to the American people and Congress:

"My fellow Americans: As President and Commander in Chief, it is my duty to the American people to report that renewed hostile actions against United States ships on the high seas in the Gulf of Tonkin have today required me to order the military forces of the United States to take action in reply.

The initial attack on the destroyer Maddox, on August 2, was repeated today by a number of hostile vessels attacking two U.S. destroyers with torpedoes. The destroyers and supporting aircraft acted at once on the orders I gave after the initial act of aggression. We believe at least two of the attacking boats were sunk. There were no U.S. losses.

The performance of commanders and crews in this engagement is in the highest tradition of the United States Navy. But repeated acts of violence against the Armed Forces of the United States must be met not only with alert defense, but with positive reply. That reply is being given as I speak to you tonight. Air action is now in execution against gunboats and certain supporting facilities in North Vietnam which have been used in these hostile operations.

In the larger sense this new act of aggression, aimed directly at our own forces, again brings home to all of us in the United States the importance of the struggle for peace and security in southeast Asia. Aggression by terror against the peaceful villagers of South Vietnam has now been joined by open aggression on the high seas against the United States of America.

The determination of all Americans to carry out our full commitment to the people and to the government of South Vietnam will be redoubled by this outrage. Yet our response, for the present, will be limited and fitting. We Americans know, although others appear to forget, the risks of spreading conflict. We still seek no wider war.

I have instructed the Secretary of State to make this position totally clear to friends and to adversaries and, indeed, to all. I have instructed Ambassador Stevenson to raise this matter immediately and urgently before the Security Council of the United Nations. Finally, I have today met with the leaders of both parties in the Congress of the United States and I have informed them that I shall immediately request the Congress to pass a resolution making it clear that our Government is united in its determination to take all necessary measures in support of freedom and in defense of peace in southeast Asia.

I have been given encouraging assurance by these leaders of both parties that such a resolution will be promptly introduced, freely and expeditiously debated, and passed with overwhelming support. And just a few minutes ago I was able to reach Senator Goldwater and I am glad to say that he has expressed his support of the statement that I am making to you tonight.

It is a solemn responsibility to have to order even limited military action by forces whose overall strength is as vast and as awesome as those of the United States of America, but it is my considered conviction, shared throughout your Government, that firmness in the right is indispensable today for peace; that firmness will always be measured. Its mission is peace."

The outcome of his efforts results in Congress immediately passing the Gulf of Tonkin Resolution, granting LBJ the authority to assist any Southeast Asian country who may be in danger from "communist aggression."

And there we have it, we are launched into a war based on a lie, costing the lives of more than 58,000 U.S. servicemen and that ultimately ended in defeat.

What is even more remarkable, is the American misunderstanding of the lies told to them about the imminent threat of "Communism." Most countries that were under what we at the time called "Communist regimes" failed by the 1980's. They failed from their bloated inefficient bureaucracies and corruption that resulted in government wasteful spending.

These countries had no chance of competing against Capitalist nations in which innovation and wealth were being created. This fact has been confirmed after the fall of the Soviet Union and it was revealed that the GDP of the U.S.S.R. was only five percent of the GDP of the U.S. Any country that chooses socialism as a path to Communism, ends up destroying wealth and impoverishing the nation. The propaganda we Americans were fed, creating fears from a Communistic threat, was completely false. There never was any threat.

Iraq 1 – The Persian Gulf War (1990-1991)

"History is written by the victors." ~**Winston Churchill**

Upon initial historical review, one may be led to believe that our involvement was righteous, and our quick victory brought pride back to our nation. However, we learn later in time after the war that our reasoning for entering was not based on truthful information. We were once again duped into putting American soldiers lives at risk for little reason.

When Saddam Hussein invaded Kuwait, there was little American interest. It was not about saving a democracy. They were essentially two kingdoms disputing rights to oil. Saddam Hussein, we were told, was the evil one, but overall, the American public did not want any involvement.

The Kuwaiti ruling Amir was about to lose the wealth of his $100 Billion-dollar Kingdom. He ran a campaign of Citizens for a Free Kuwait to drum up American support for a US-led invasion. Kuwaiti expatriates contacted the major public relations firm Hill & Knowlton to lead the campaign. Their efforts began with conducting focus groups to determine the best strategy to winning the support of the Americans. Many believe that President Bush was briefed continuously on their progress. Up to this point, news only trickled out about the Iraqi invasion.

That all changed when a story broke September 2, 1990, that Iraqi soldiers were taking babies out of incubators and leaving them on the floor to die in order to send the incubators back to Iraq. Their actions resulted in the deaths of hundreds of premature babies. The Washington Post ran with the story even though they were unable to verify its truthfulness.

NPR's, *All Things Considered,* had an interview with a Kuwaiti hostage stating that the Iraqi soldiers were "hitting children with the butts of the guns, taking infants out of incubators and taking the incubators."

Nayirah al-Ṣabaḥ during her testimony
National Cable Satellite Corporation (C-SPAN), public domain, via Wikimedia Commons

Hill & Knowlton prepared a fifteen-year-old Kuwaiti girl, Nayirah, who claimed to be a witness to testify before a congressional hearing. She was brought before the U.S. Congress to testify on October 10, 1990.

Her statement read as follows:

"Mr. Chairman, and members of the committee, my name is Nayirah and I just came out of Kuwait. My mother and I were in Kuwait on August 2nd for a peaceful summer holiday. My older sister had a baby on July 29th and we wanted to spend some time in Kuwait with her.

I only pray that none of my 10th grade classmates had a summer vacation like I did. I may have wished sometimes that I can be an adult, that I could grow up quickly. What I saw happening to the children of Kuwait and to my country has changed my life forever, has changed the life of all Kuwaitis, young and old, mere children or more.

My sister with my five-day-old nephew traveled across the desert to safety. There is no milk available for the baby in Kuwait. They barely escaped when their car was stuck in the desert sand and help came from Saudi Arabia.

I stayed behind and wanted to do something for my country. The second week after invasion, I volunteered at the AlIdar Hospital with 12 other women who wanted to help as well. I was the youngest volunteer. The "other" women were from 20 to 30 years old.

While I was there, I saw the Iraqi soldiers come into the hospital with guns. They took the babies out of the incubators, took the incubators and left the children to die on the cold floor. It was horrifying. I could not help but think of my nephew who was born premature and might have died that day as well. After I left the hospital, some of my friends and I distributed flyers condemning the Iraqi invasion until we were warned we might be killed if the Iraqis saw us.

The Iraqis have destroyed everything in Kuwait. They stripped the supermarkets of food, the pharmacies of medicine, the factories of medical supplies, ransacked their houses and tortured neighbors and friends.

I saw and talked to a friend of mine after his torture and release by the Iraqis. He is 22 but he looked as though he could have been an old man. The Iraqis dunked his head into a swimming pool until he almost drowned. They pulled out his fingernails and then played [sic] electric shocks to sensitive private parts of his body. He was lucky to survive.

If an Iraqi soldier is found dead in the neighborhood, they burn to the ground all the houses in the general vicinity and would not let firefighters come until the only ash and rubble was left.

The Iraqis were making fun of President Bush and verbally and physically abusing my family and me on our way out of Kuwait. We only did so because life in Kuwait became unbearable. They have forced us to hide, burn or destroy everything identifying our country and our government.

I want to emphasize that Kuwait is our mother and the Emir our father. We repeated this on the roofs of our houses in Kuwait until the Iraqis began shooting at us, and we shall repeat it again. I am glad I am 15, old enough to remember Kuwait before Saddam Hussein destroyed it and young enough to rebuild it

Thank you."
~ Nayirah Al-Sabah, 1990

Millions of Americans were glued to the coverage of the hearing. They were angered by such actions. President Bush repeated the story multiple times in the following weeks. Immediately following, military support was approved, and President Bush worked to launch the Persian Gulf War.

Later in 1992, after the war is over, we learned that Nayirah was the daughter of the Kuwaiti Ambassador. We learned that yes, medical equipment was taken, but nothing to the degree described in the testimonies. We know this for a fact because after the war when we went into the hospitals, the equipment was still there untouched.

There were investigations into the story as well by the human rights organization Middle East Watch, which is a division of Human Rights Watch. The director, Andrew Whitley, stated to the press, "While it is true that the Iraqis targeted hospitals, there is no truth to the charge which was central to the war propaganda effort that they stole incubators and callously removed babies allowing them to die on the floor. The stories were manufactured from germs of truth by people outside the country who should have known better."

We do know that the Iraqis looted equipment and committed many crimes when invading the country, but not in the form and extent sold to the American people. Hill & Knowlton knew they found a successful public relations campaign that would persuade the Americans to go to war. The Kuwaiti Amir had his Kingdom restored, all based on a lie.

Iraq 2 – The Invasion (2003-2011)

"No man's life, liberty, or property are safe while Congress is in session." ~**Mark Twain**

We should by this point know how to discern propaganda from truth or at least begin to question it. We are by the year 2000 an advanced society with access to many forms of news media including the internet. We have a society with the most education in the history of the world. How could we possibly be duped into another war based on lies?

At this time, we are a nation still in fear of a terrorist threat. Having just recovered from the 9/11 attacks, the media pounds the drum of war to take revenge on those attackers. President George W. Bush leads us to believe that Saddam Hussein has Weapons of Mass Destruction (WMDs). As he works to gain support from European countries, France, England and Germany to invade, the European nation's own investigations conclude that the WMD's don't exist. Even as late as February 2003, the IAEA stated, they "found no evidence or plausible indication of the revival of a nuclear weapons program in Iraq."

Powell holds vial with Anthrax February 5, 2003
Public domain, via Wikimedia Commons

On February 5, 2003, Secretary of State, Colin L. Powell, speaks before the United Nations Security Council stating that he had evidence that Iraq does have WMDs and that they were being hidden from the weapons inspectors. During his speech he even holds up a model vial of Anthrax.

Excerpts from his speech:

"My second purpose today is ... to share with you what the United States knows about Iraq's weapons of mass destruction ... Iraq's behavior demonstrate that Saddam Hussein and his regime have made no effort ... to disarm as required by the international community. Indeed, the facts and Iraq's behavior show that Saddam Hussein and his regime are concealing their efforts to produce more weapons of mass destruction ... every

statement I make today is backed up by sources, solid sources. These are not assertions. What we're giving you are facts and conclusions based on solid intelligence.

Numerous human sources tell us that the Iraqis are moving not just documents and hard drives, but weapons of mass destruction, to keep them from being found by inspectors. While we were here in this Council chamber debating Resolution 1441 last fall, we know, we know from sources that a missile brigade outside Baghdad was dispersing rocket launchers and warheads containing biological warfare agent to various locations, distributing them to various locations in western Iraq.

Most of the launchers and warheads had been hidden in large groves of palm trees and were to be moved every one to four weeks to escape detection.

We also have satellite photos that indicate that banned materials have recently been moved from a number of Iraqi weapons of mass destruction facilities.

Let me say a word about satellite images before I show a couple. The photos that I am about to show you are sometimes hard for the average person to interpret, hard for me. The painstaking work of photo analysis takes experts with years and years of experience, poring for hours and hours over light tables. But as I show you these images, I will try to capture and explain what they mean, what they indicate, to our imagery specialists.

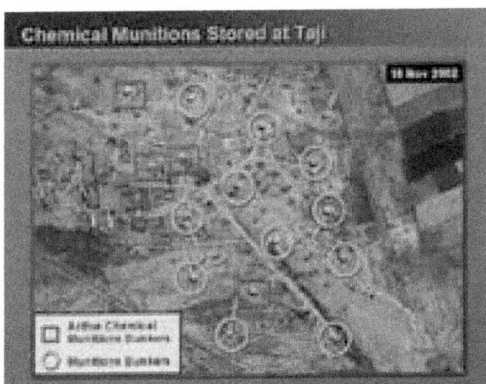
Chemical Munitions Stored at Taji

Let's look at one. This one is about a weapons munition facility, a facility that holds ammunition at a place called Taji. This is one of about 65 such facilities in Iraq. We know that this one has housed chemical munitions. In fact, this is where the Iraqis recently came up with the additional four chemical weapons shells.

Here you see 15 munitions bunkers in yellow and red outlines. The four that are in red squares

Sanitization of Ammunition Depot at Taji

represent active chemical munitions bunkers.

How do I know that? How can I say that? Let me give you a closer look. Look at the image on the left. On the left is a close-up of one of the four chemical bunkers. The two arrows indicate the presence of sure signs that the bunkers are storing chemical munitions. The arrow at the top that says "security" points to a facility that is a signature item for this kind of

- 59 -

bunker. Inside that facility are special guards and special equipment to monitor any leakage that might come out of the bunker. The truck you also see is a signature item. It's a decontamination vehicle in case something goes wrong. This is characteristic of those four bunkers. The special security facility and the decontamination vehicle will be in the area, if not at any one of them or one of the other, it is moving around those four and it moves as needed to move as people are working in the different bunkers.

Now look at the picture on the right. You are now looking at two of those sanitized bunkers. The signature vehicles are gone, the tents are gone. It's been cleaned up. And it was done on the 22nd of December as the UN inspection team is arriving, and you can see the inspection vehicles arriving in the lower portion of the picture on the right.
The bunkers are clean when the inspectors get there. They found nothing.

This sequence of events raises the worrisome suspicion that Iraq had been tipped off to the forthcoming inspections at Taji. As it did throughout the 1990s, we know that Iraq today is actively using its considerable intelligence capabilities to hide its illicit activities. From our sources, we know that inspectors are under constant surveillance by an army of Iraqi intelligence operatives. Iraq is relentlessly attempting to tap all of their communications, both voice and electronics. I would call my colleagues' attention to the fine paper that the United Kingdom distributed yesterday which describes in exquisite detail Iraqi deception activities.

In this next example, you will see the type of

Pre-Inspection Al Fatah Missile Removal
Al-Musayyib Rocket Test Facility

concealment activity Iraq has undertaken in response to the resumption of inspections. Indeed, in November of 2002, just when the inspections were about to resume, this type of activity spiked. Here are three examples.

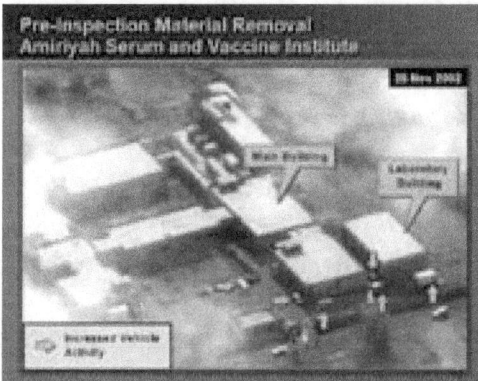

Pre-Inspection Material Removal
Amiriyah Serum and Vaccine Institute

At this ballistic missile site on November 10th, we saw a cargo truck preparing to move ballistic missile components. At this biological weapons-related facility on November 25th, just two days before inspections resumed, this truck caravan appeared -- something we almost never see at this facility and we monitor it carefully and regularly.

At this ballistic missile facility, again, two days before inspections began, five large cargo trucks

Pre-Inspection Materiel Removal, Ibn al Haytham

appeared, along with a truck-mounted crane, to move missiles.

We saw this kind of housecleaning at close to 30 sites. Days after this activity, the vehicles and the equipment that I've just highlighted disappear and the site returns to patterns of normalcy. We don't know precisely what Iraq was moving, but the inspectors already knew about these sites so Iraq knew that they would be coming.

We must ask ourselves: Why would Iraq suddenly move equipment of this nature before inspections if they were anxious to demonstrate what they had or did not have?

Remember the first intercept in which two Iraqis talked about the need to hide a modified vehicle from the inspectors. Where did Iraq take all of this equipment? Why wasn't it presented to the inspectors?"

As documented on the website: https://201-2009.state.gov/secretary/former/powell/remarks/2003/17173.htm

Up to this point in time, Colin Powell was respected and trusted by the American public. Another leader making these statements would not of had the same impact. Almost every American listening to Powell speak believed what he was reporting. There was little doubt and the news media took the story and ran with it. Americans were afraid of Saddam and were now prepared to go to war to stop his imminent threat. When Congress voted, they voted for war, and there was little debate or opposition.

As we invaded the country it didn't take long to realize that there were no WMDs to be found. All of Powell's details as to the locations were false. We occupied the country for 14 years and we never found any evidence of WMDs. The invasion and occupation resulted in the deaths of over 600,000 people, including as many as 200,000 civilians. The region was destabilized. To this day, Iraq has failed to keep a stable government. Saddam was able to keep Iran in check and unify Iraq. Now we have tribal rule and the ISIS risk of terrorism is real. When Saddam was in charge there were no terrorist threats in Iraq.

As the war rages on for years, Americans came to the realization that WMDs did not exist, but they were told not to worry as the narrative for justifying our invasion changed. We all began to believe that control of the supply of oil was justified to continue our efforts to secure a favorable Iraqi government based on democracy. This remains in the back of most Americans' minds to this day.

The reality is, whoever or whatever form of government exists, these oil producing countries will be willing to cooperate to sell oil on the open markets. They need us as customers.

Afghanistan - The Global War on Terrorism Begins (2001-2021)

The shock of the 9/11 attacks, an attack on American soil, sends the public into a frenzy for revenge. We must hunt down those that organized the attack and bring them to justice. Shortly afterwards, the American Coalition led 40 countries, including all of the NATO Alliance, to occupy Afghanistan, kicking off the global war on terror.

Osama bin Laden
Assumed to be Bin Laden or associates, public domain, via Wikimedia Commons

As Osama bin Laden is being hunted in Afghanistan, we recover a letter on an al Qaeda computer from bin Laden to the Taliban leadership:

"All that we have to do is to send two mujahideen to the furthest point east to raise a piece of cloth on which is written al Qaeda, in order to make generals race there to cause America to suffer human, economic and political losses without their achieving anything of note other than some benefits for their private corporations. This is in addition to our having

experience in using guerrilla warfare and the war of attrition to fight tyrannical superpowers, as we, alongside the mujahideen, bled Russia for 10 years, until it went bankrupt and was forced to withdraw in defeat. ... So, we are continuing this policy of bleeding America to the point of bankruptcy."

~Osama bin Laden
("Fool's Errand" by Scott Horton, 2017, p48)

The mainstream media pounds the drum of war, ignoring the fact that the Taliban had no part in the 9/11 attacks. As the Taliban refuse to cooperate with the hunt for bin Laden, President George W. Bush and the media convince the public and politicians that we must invade the country. The reasoning drifts from hunting bin Laden, to eliminating al Qaeda training camps, to fighting for the rights of women in the Afghan culture. We begin a 20-year, $3.5 Trillion nation building effort to create a "Democracy" in a country led by tribal war lords.

Below is a link to Congressman Ron Paul's speech on March 17, 2011, before the U.S. House of Representatives making the case to end the war immediately. The war, at that point, had dragged on for a decade with no results and no end in sight. There was a brief moment in early 2011 of political pressure to end the war. He stated, "we should leave by the end of the year and if we don't, we will be there for another decade." Unfortunately, Ron Paul's efforts failed, however he is later proven right when we finally pull out in August of 2021.

Bonus Food for Thought:

On May 2, 2011, it is announced that the leader of al Qaeda, Osama bin Laden, is killed.

Did Navy SEAL Team 6 really kill Osama bin Laden in 2011?

What remains odd is why such an elite military team was not able to capture him alive. They killed him unarmed and defenseless. There is very little evidence of his death being presented to the public. Even to this day, there are no photos, videos or bodies. It would have been a great victory to bring him back to the US to face a trial in front of the world. What a great moment that would have been in the War on Terror. We need to ask ourselves, "would our President, Barack Hussein Obama, fake the assassination for political gain?"

Unfortunately, three months later, on December 11, 2015, fifteen commandos from the same SEAL Team 6 die in a helicopter crash from a supposedly Taliban attack. The black box is never recovered, said to have been washed away in a flash flood a short time after the crash. The U.S. government has never confirmed if they were the same commandos on the mission to kill bin Laden. There are many questions left unanswered.

"Dead men tell no tales."

American Soldiers in Tora Bora, Afghanistan
Rick Scavetta, public domain, via Wikimedia Commons

Congressman Ron Paul's speech on March 17, 2011, before the U.S. House of Representatives

https://www.youtube.com/watch?v=GrHm4phj5RQ

While the mainstream media ignores the coverage of the war, in 2017 Scott Horton's excellent book, "Fool's Errand" explains and captures the lies and hypocrisy of one of our nation's longest running wars. In 2021, the US finally pulls out, leaving behind over

176,000 dead of which 46,000 were civilians and displacing over 6.6 million people.

Continuing the Global War on Terrorism: Somalia, Libya, Syria, Yemen, & Pakistan

World Map

After the invasion of Afghanistan, our military continued to expand its campaign against terrorism. At one point in President Obama's administration, with Hillary Clinton as Secretary of State, the U.S. was drone bombing seven countries: Afghanistan, Pakistan, Iraq, Somalia, Libya, Syria and Yemen. The Middle East was destabilized. The more we fought terrorism, the more terrorists there were. ISIS came to power. Hatred and anger against U.S. foreign intervention deepened across the region.

The media pounded the war drums explaining our actions with relatively little coverage of the human death toll and atrocities committed. In Syria, we were told King Assad used chemical weapons, which to this day has been disputed as a false flag event. In Libya, we were told that Muammar Kaddafi is an evil dictator also threatening use of chemical weapons. We toppled his government, but the people remain in chaos and on the verge of civil war to this day.

In Yemen, a war rages against Saudi Arabia. The coverage from the media is almost non-existent. The U.S. supplies weapons to the House of Saud, the Kingdom of Saudi Arabia, which in turn are used against Yemen. Most Americans do not know that the Saudi Kingdom does not have its own military. The Kingdom knows well from history that arming their own military would put their power at risk. They would risk a military general in charge of seizing power from them. Using their oil wealth, they are able to pay the U.S. to supply the military for them. The UN estimates over 200,000 have died from war and famine in Yemen. More than a million continue to suffer in a horrific famine as the U.S. government spends billions of dollars in military aid to the House of Saud.

Today our military budget, over $800 Billion, exceeds the budgets of all other countries in the world combined! We have bases in over 700 locations. Drones drop bombs indiscriminately on soldiers and civilians. The media ignores the coverage, "lying through omission," to ensure that the U.S. public is unaware. If the people knew the truth about the War on Terror, they would protest and put a stop to it.

Today the War on Terror has now expanded to include a new phrase, "Domestic terrorist." If you are someone who challenges the narrative of the State, you will now be at risk of being labeled a domestic terrorist.

Bonus Food for Thought:

Why is it that some countries with kings and dictators such as Saudi Arabia, the U.A.E., and Kuwait are not threatened with sanctions and are left alone from U.S. intervention, while other countries such as Venezuela, Russia, Iraq, Iran, Libya and Syria are either under attack or heavily sanctioned. The Americans seem to have forgotten that the terrorists flying the planes in 9/11 were Saudis. Is the motive to spread democracy or remove terrorist threats? For example, we know almost with certainty that there were no terrorists in Iraq before the invasion. Saddam Hussein would not tolerate it. His country was very stable. To this day, there are no terrorists in Venezuela.

One theory is that the leaders of these unfavored countries don't cooperate with the U.S. dollar trading in the market. The dollar is used in 90% of foreign exchange transactions throughout the world. For this reason, the U.S. dollar maintains its dollar hegemony. Countries that attempt to threaten this system and trade without U.S. dollars are immediately understood to be uncooperative with the U.S. Saddam Hussein of Iraq, Muammar Kaddafi of Libya, Hugo Chavez of Venezuela, and Vladimir Putin of Russia all publicly stated over time plans to trade outside the U.S. dollar. The U.S. understands the meaning of this threat and works to destroy them. Leadership must get in line or be replaced.

Ukraine – A Proxy War for the U.S. and Russia

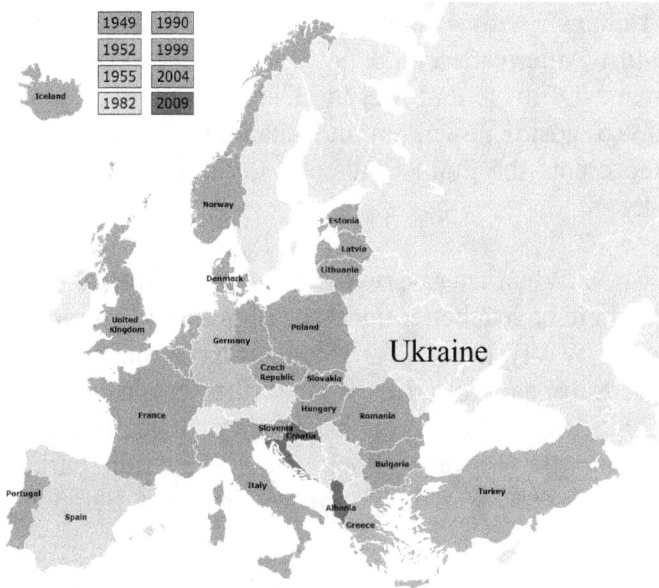

1949	1990
1952	1999
1955	2004
1982	2009

NATO Expansion

Wikimedia Commons, the free media repository.
https://commons.wikimedia.org/w/index.php?title=File:NATO_expansion.png&oldid=6
90297948

Despite the fact that the U.S. is not directly at war with Russia yet, Ukraine has become a proxy war. The U.S. has again drummed up support to fund supplies to defend Ukraine in the name of freedom and democracy. At the time of this writing, over $60 billion in military aid has been sent. To put this in perspective, this is as much as the entire annual Russian defense budget. Russia continues to gain territory as the country is destroyed and its citizens are displaced.

"History doesn't repeat itself, but it often rhymes." ~**Mark Twain**

The media rages that President Vladimir Putin is evil, and his aggression must be stopped. The fear "rhymes" with Hitler's invasion of Czechoslovakia. Most Americans could not even place Ukraine on a map. Of those that tout the Ukrainian flag, they often do so upside down, not understanding the yellow color represents the grain fields and the blue represents the sky.

When we review the history of Ukraine, we can begin to have a better understanding of Putin's motives. After WWII, the NATO alliance was formed to protect the European countries from further expansion of the U.S.S.R. as Stalin expanded into Eastern Europe, putting the Eastern Block under the "iron curtain." NATO represented the armed nuclear defense of Western Europe.

Ukraine On Fire, Documentary by Oliver Stone

https://www.youtube.com/watch?v=IwZApPCFXIc

In 1991 the U.S.S.R. collapses, the Berlin wall came down, and the U.S.S.R. breaks up into independent countries. Eastern European countries are given their independence from Russia, however many of the governments established maintain close ties to the

Russian government. At that time, the US, England and France promises that NATO will not expand into these newly formed countries. The promise is short lived.

In the late 1990's, President Bill Clinton begins to expand NATO. By 2020 as noted in the map above, NATO has expanded into 14 countries. As NATO expands, so do nuclear weapons. Russia, concerned that nuclear weapons in Kiev would not allow enough Russian response time if launched against Moscow, has asked repeatedly for President Biden to guarantee that that Ukraine will not join NATO. Biden refuses to agree and Putin immediately invades.

Putin is cornered to respond, fearing that the West's nuclear weapons will be too close to Moscow, threatening his country. Russia has always viewed the Eastern European countries as a buffer since WWII. They fear that there is always a possibility of another invasion from Europe as they suffered greatly during WWII. It would be as if Russia took control of the Mexican government and then installed nuclear weapons there. Americans would immediately call for war, just as we threatened during the Cuban missile crisis of 1962.

Do we really need NATO at this point? It is a relic of the cold war. Do we need to weaponize Eastern European countries with nuclear missiles? Are we really protecting a democracy, when even the Heritage Foundation's ranking of economic freedom shows that the Ukraine is less free than Russia itself? How much are the military defense contractors profiting from the boom in arms sales to defend a potentially highly corrupt government under President Volodymyr Zelenskyy? Are we being fed another war lie?

Revealing Ukraine, **Documentary by Oliver Stone**

https://www.youtube.com/watch?v=9E9i24XhWtw

Bonus Food for Thought:

Is the real threat from Putin his statements that the U.S. dollar hegemonic power is a problem for the world's nations? Russia is working with China and other BRIC nations to move off the dollar standard. Their efforts to trade in currencies other than the U.S. dollar could be understood as more of a threat than the invasion of Ukraine. In comparison to similar statements from Saddam, Kaddafi and Chavez, is the West also trying to topple Putin?

America's War on Drugs

Figure 1. National Drug-Involved Overdose Deaths*
Number Among All Ages, by Gender, 1999-2020

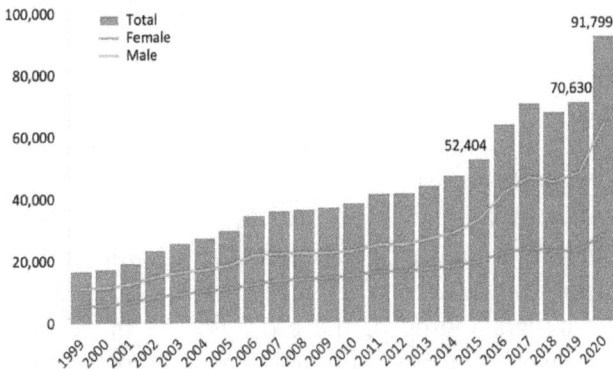

*Includes deaths with underlying causes of unintentional drug poisoning (X40–X44), suicide drug poisoning (X60–X64), homicide drug poisoning (X85), or drug poisoning of undetermined intent (Y10–Y14), as coded in the International Classification of Diseases, 10th Revision. Source: Centers for Disease Control and Prevention, National Center for Health Statistics. Multiple Cause of Death: 1999-2020 on CDC WONDER Online Database, released 12/2021.

National Institute on Drug Abuse. User: Time shifter. Public domain, via Wikimedia Commons

By 2021, America breaks new records annually for deaths from drug overdoses after almost a century of fighting the drug war. 2021's death toll exceeds more than 107,000. We would think that by this time it is apparent we are losing the War on Drugs. We need to all ask ourselves are we doing something wrong in our society? Methamphetamines and Fentanyl pore into the country. The streets of major cities are littered with homeless camps in which drug distribution is rampant.

The cost to the American taxpayer on a federal level has been more than one $US Trillion dollars since 1971. Currently the Federal budget in 2022 is $US 41 billion, however the true cost is estimated at exceeding $US100 Billion annually when considering State and local governments expenses including the cost of incarceration. America now has a higher percentage of its population incarcerated than Stalin did in the U.S.S.R. With two million incarcerations, we imprison more people than any other country in the world. Paradoxically, marijuana's use across the country is commonplace and employers struggle to find employees drug free. How did we get into this mess?

In the late 1800's, morphine was a drug used as a painkiller and of which a small percentage of the population was addicted. At this time drugs were not illegal nor was drug abuse a problem. Opium, heroin, and morphine were easily accessible. There was also little understanding of these drugs. As the Teetotaler movement escalated, opium was prescribed to cure alcoholism. Subsequently, morphine was prescribed to cure opium addiction and soon after heroin was a cure for morphine addiction. Later, methadone was used to cure heroin addiction. None of which worked.

The first drug laws passed in San Francisco in 1875 were racist in origin, targeting opium use of which was more common by the Chinese. The local labor unions did not want to compete against the Chinese and worked to pass anti-immigration laws as well as use of opium. The AFL labor union led by Samuel Gompers successfully passed the first US drug law with the intent to racially discriminate against Chinese laborers.

It wasn't until 1914 that Congress passes the Harrison Narcotics Act. Up to that time, we as a nation still did not have any drug problem. Immediately, just as when prohibition started, the cost of the drugs increased. The supply chain goes underground and as prices continue to escalate users begin to turn to crime to maintain their habits. In 1937, the Marijuana Tax Act is passed by Congress, making passage and transportation illegal on a federal level. From that point on, the drug problem in the U.S. only grows. More laws are added on the books, and as costs continue to rise to supply the users, crime levels rise, police forces grow and prisons fill.

The story of drug use escalation can simply be explained through an economic understanding of businesses providing a product to a market for profit. In 1973, Rockefeller Drug Laws go into effect, enacting harsh prison sentences for drug offenses. America escalates its War on Drugs, which officially kicked off in 1961.

Prior to this period, the drugs used were mainly heroin and marijuana. However, as police and Federal drug agencies crack down on traffickers, they find it more difficult to transport bales of marijuana. They needed a product that was more condensed. Hence, cocaine comes to the market in the 1970s. However, as the DEA continues to fight the traffickers, they again looked to a more improved product, hence crack cocaine hits the streets of the U.S. in the 1980s. In the 90's and into the 2000s, synthetic drugs. Ultimately, we end up with the drugs used today, methamphetamines and Fentanyl. In each step of this cycle the products are easier to transport, however more powerful and addictive.

Australian-Afghan Army Patrol April 2010
During the U.S. occupation of Afghanistan, poppy seed farming and heroin production explodes to fund the Taliban's army.

Over a period of 100 years, we go from using relatively harmless drugs, morphine and opium, to drugs that are so powerful that even accidentally breathing in the dust can kill. As with the bootleggers during prohibition, a dangerous corrupt trafficking network is developed throughout the world of which no government is capable of stopping. Millions have been charged with felonies and incarcerated, leaving lives and families ruined. Our court system is choked handling the cases. Governments of developing nations throughout the world are corrupted from the drug trade. In countries like Mexico, Columbia, and Pakistan, the drug war rages, creating the most dangerous places to live on our planet. The outcome of over 60 years of the War on Drugs focusing on attacking and limiting supply has only resulted in a more complex supply and distribution system managed by sophisticated cartels. Their dangerous products become more addictive and lethal. The demand in our society only increases.

The hypocrisy of states legalizing and taxing marijuana use only makes it even clearer that this is a war only to end in defeat. All the while, Federal and State governments are calling for increasing police forces, building more prisons, and mandating harsher punishments. In comparison to most 3rd world developing nations, the drug problem is mainly a problem of Western nations. In developing nations, it is common to observe the occasional overuse of alcohol, but rarely do you even hear about a drug problem. Drugs are often a problem near hotels where Western foreigners visit. No cities exist outside the U.S. like San Francisco or New York where you see large numbers of people stoned in the streets living in tent cities.

The story of the drug user becomes the saddest. As the price rises, they need to turn to a life of crime to maintain their addictive habit. To purchase $100 worth of drugs, they may need to steal $500 worth of goods to earn the street value. They turn to prostitution in desperation. Other expenses, such as food and housing, are neglected, resulting in malnutrition, sickness and homelessness. Their criminal records prevent them from ever returning to society as productive citizens. Not employable for life, they become parasites through government spending programs on the rest of society.

"If one abolishes man's freedom to determine his own consumption, then one takes all freedoms away." ~**Ludwig Van Mises,** Human *Action*

Bonus Food for Thought:

Detroit Police During Prohibition
Unknown author: Public domain, via Wikimedia Commons

There is no better story to explain the failure of the War on Drugs than to review the history of Prohibition. In 1919, the 18th Amendment to the U.S. Constitution is passed prohibiting the production, importation, transportation, and sale of alcohol. Interestingly, the consumption of alcohol is not banned. Congressmen knew that banning consumption was not a good idea, because then they would need to stop drinking as well, and they obviously didn't want that.

As the laws went into effect, businessmen understood that even though the law was focused on the supply to the consumer, the demand remained. They quickly found solutions to bring the alcohol to the market. As a result, rampant crime arose in order to maintain the supply to the market as police turned a blind eye through bribery. Sales and distribution were controlled by dangerous gang organizations, often battling it out to maintain their market share. Famous mobsters such as Al Capone, Lucky Luciano, Bugs Moran, Joseph Bonanno, Joseph Kennedy (father of President John F. Kennedy), became the news of the day. All unintended consequences of the legislation.

Over time, the people came to realize the prohibition laws had no impact on society. The bootleggers were making fortunes all across the U.S. as they took control of an industry for profit. The laws were impossible to regulate and in 1933, the 21st Amendment was passed to repeal the 18th Amendment.

Bonus Food for Thought:

Cannabis Sativa Tree

In passing of the Marijuana Tax Act of 1937, slipped into the legislation by the Du Pont family, was a heavy tax on hemp production. Hemp had no use as a drug or narcotic, however as a plant, it is similar in that it is from the class Cannabis Sativa. As a fiber used worldwide, its primary use was in paper, rope, textiles and clothing.

Why would a product that was not a drug like its marijuana cousin be included in this law? When reviewing the history, there were several powerful businessmen looking out for their own interests. Andrew Mellon, Secretary of the Treasury at the time, was heavily invested in the Du Pont's nylon business. The Du Pont's nylon product was directly in competition with the rope, textile and clothing industry. William Randolph Hearst realized that the rise in hemp production, a product used for pulp and paper, would compete against his timber business which supplied the paper industry needed for newspapers. These men knew that by squashing the hemp industry with a heavy tax, they would gain control of major world markets.

By 1970, the passage of the Controlled Substances Act ultimately made the production of industrial hemp illegal as part of the U.S. War on Drugs. It was not until 2018 that hemp was legalized again.

America's War on Poverty

"The problem with Socialism and Socialists is they keep running out of other people's money."
~**Margaret Thatcher**

America's War on Poverty kicked off under President Lyndon B. Johnson's administration with the intention of creating a Great Society. In reality, the programs were only an extension of President Franklin D. Roosevelt's New Deal program focused on eradicating poverty across the U.S. Why not, as we were at that time an extremely wealthy nation. No American should suffer as there was plenty of wealth to go around. During this period of time, these programs drastically expanded government's role in Americans lives. As Americans passed their responsibilities on to the government for care, they now pay for its unintended consequences.

"Nothing is so permanent as a temporary government program." ~**Milton Friedman**

For starters, the Social Security program, was expanded to include Medicare and Medicaid intended to care for the elderly. Americans believing that as they pay into this program over their working lives, they would not need to worry about health care in retirement. "Big Brother" would be there to take care of them. Over the decades, as the fund grew and the government fell further and further into debt, the fund was ultimately raided. Currently this program with Social Security is underfunded by $US 56 trillion. To make matters worse, the monthly payments that the citizens receive are no longer adequate. The erosion of the U.S. dollar's value didn't keep up with the rising cost of living. Americans were duped.

Bonus Food for Thought:

When I was younger, working overseas in a poor country in the early 2000s, the country's government was implementing a new Social Security system modeling the U.S. system. As I was amongst friends, I shared my opinion that I thought that it would be a good program for the people. At that time in my life, I had little understanding of these programs. Everyone stopped talking and began laughing. I couldn't understand why. They all clearly understood that they were never going to see that money. It was all going to be looted or given back to them as worthless paper.

In addition, as Americans believed that the government will care for them in old age, their children relinquished their responsibility to care for them. The culture changed and now the elderly are quickly put into nursing homes left to die alone. The nuclear family is destroyed as a result of socialist policies. In most countries throughout the world where there are no social security programs, the family takes the responsibility of caring for its elders.

The Food Stamp program was initiated to ensure poor families did not go hungry. Over time, as those on this program didn't pay for their food, expensive junk food became a major part of their diets. Obesity becomes a severe health problem for the poor in the U.S.

The Elementary and Secondary Education Act expanded federal funding of public schools. After decades of bloated school budgets, which often run at a higher cost per student than many private schools, there are no results to show for it. Our Nation's testing scores have only continued to decline for decades. As the educational programs are dumbed down, high numbers of students graduate unable to read or write.

Welfare programs for single mothers again begin with good intentions to help those who fell on hard times. However, Americans on welfare remained on welfare. We now have three generations of welfare. Divorce rates escalated as the role of the father in the household to care for the family was no longer required. Fathers could easily leave, and the mothers would receive support from the State, becoming a core reason for the destruction of the nuclear family amongst America's poor.

"The nine most terrifying words in the English language are: I'm from the government and I'm here to help." ~**President Ronald Reagan**

Although not part of the programs of the Great Society, but implemented with the same mindset at the time, was the expansion of rent control laws nationwide. Because rent controls often apply to buildings constructed before a certain date, older buildings are no longer torn down to construct taller buildings able to house more tenants. Tenants in rent-controlled apartments know the value and hold onto them for as long as possible. The result over decades is that builders no longer build new. The business is no longer profitable. Over time, a shortage in housing develops, resulting in escalating rents for those outside of rent-controlled areas and homelessness for others. It is very interesting to note that in most third world countries, homelessness is non-existent. The reason is there are no rent control nor zoning laws. The free market finds a way to build affordable homes for all citizens.

"Unfortunately, the real minimum wage is always zero, regardless of the laws, and that is the wage that many workers receive in the wake of the creation or escalation of a government-mandated minimum wage, because they lose their jobs or fail to find jobs when they enter the labor force. Making it illegal to pay less than a given amount does not make a worker's productivity worth that amount—and, if it is not, that worker is unlikely to be employed." ~**Thomas Sowell, Basic Economics: A Citizen's Guide to the Economy**

Minimum wage laws continue to be implemented and rise during this period as well. Politicians can always earn votes by offering to raise the minimum wage laws. On the surface it sounds great to force those evil profit driven companies to pay their workers a better salary. What is missed is those jobs paid below the new minimum wage are eliminated. Those jobs no longer bring value and businesses find ways to permanently eliminate them. Examples, such as improved automation, stronger computer programs, or even relocating the jobs overseas is required to keep the businesses profitable. Those jobs never return.

"A strong man cannot help a weaker unless the weaker is willing to be helped, and even then, the weak man must become strong of himself; he must, by his own efforts, develop the strength which he admires in another. None but himself can alter his condition." **~James Allen, "As a Man Thinketh"**

The funding of the Vietnam War and the Great Society programs became the precursor to the high inflation of the 1970's. Ironically, the intention to build a Great Society resulted in the National debt accelerating, beginning the process of impoverishing our nation. None of the problems the programs of Great Society intended to solve were ever improved.

In fact, over the last 50 years, the problems have only been magnified. As Americans, we have gone from the wealthiest, most powerful nation on Earth to the most indebted. The U.S. has not been able to win any of its wars, Korean, Vietnam, Persian Gulf, Afghanistan, Iraq 2, War on Terror, War on Drugs, nor the War on Poverty for over 75 years.

America's Health

As citizens, we are led to believe that we have the best medical care in the world. Only when traveling outside the U.S., does one begin to realize this is not the case. Yes, we have many great doctors, medicines, and amazing trauma centers. At what cost? What level of care exists in other parts of the world?

From a broader perspective, the quality, ease, and cost of health care leaves a lot to be desired when compared to most other countries. If you need emergency room care, you will be easily waiting for 6-10 hours before a doctor will see you. It is difficult to book appointments with Primary care physicians. Specialist appointments often require months of wait time.

When you finally see a doctor, they treat you like cattle. They are quick to send you for a litany of exams, most of which are unnecessary, needed only to protect themselves from a lawsuit. You are only part of the money-making machine. True care that fixes the root of your symptoms is neglected. You are given prescriptions only to relieve the symptoms and then scheduled for the next visit.

The American Medical Association (AMA) works carefully to regulate and limit the number of doctors entering the medical field each year. They understand that if there are too many doctors, their price for service would decline. Over decades of careful admittance controls, we end up with a shortage of physicians in all fields. Society suffers from a lack of care. The AMA is a powerful organization acting as a union organizer instead of using a free market approach.

If students are capable and willing, they should be admitted. If the situation ever does arise when there are too many physicians and the work does not pay well, they will find other work or choose other professions.

In most countries throughout the world, this is not the case. The medical schools take in all students who qualify and apply. In turn, there is an abundance of medical professionals able to meet the needs of the population. The cost for medical care is a fraction of the cost in the U.S. Also, due to the level of competition, the care given to the individual is higher.

Upon graduation, all doctors swear to the Hippocratic Oath:

"I swear to fulfill, to the best of my ability and judgment, this covenant:

I will respect the hard-won scientific gains of those physicians in whose steps I walk, and gladly share such knowledge as is mine with those who are to follow.

I will apply, for the benefit of the sick, all measures that are required, avoiding those twin traps of overtreatment and therapeutic nihilism.

I will remember that there is art to medicine as well as science, and that warmth, sympathy, and understanding may outweigh the surgeon's knife or the chemist's drug.

I will not be ashamed to say "I know not," nor will I fail to call in my colleagues when the skills of another are needed for a patient's recovery.

I will respect the privacy of my patients, for their problems are not disclosed to me that the world may know. Most especially must I tread with care in matters of life and death. If it is given me to save a life, all thanks. But it may also be within my power to take a life; this awesome responsibility must be faced with great humbleness and awareness of my own frailty. Above all, I must not play at God.

I will remember that I do not treat a fever chart, a cancerous growth, but a sick human being, whose illness may affect the person's family and economic stability. My responsibility includes these related problems, if I am to care adequately for the sick.

I will prevent disease whenever I can, for prevention is preferable to cure.

I will remember that I remain a member of society, with special obligations to all my fellow human beings, those sound of mind and body as well as the infirm.

If I do not violate this oath, may I enjoy life and art, respected while I live and remembered with affection thereafter. May I always act so as to preserve the finest traditions of my calling and may I long experience the joy of healing those who seek my help."

~**Louis Lasagna**

We need to ask, do physicians honor this pledge?

Most damaging to the patients is the tie between Pharma and the medical professionals. It is hard to observe the legions of Pharma's slick salespersons meeting with the physicians on a regular basis to promote their products. Offering golf trips and other benefits in trade for prescribing their products to their patients. The physicians accepting these benefits are compromised with Pharma leaving the patient at risk.

The Insys scandal captures how the physician and Pharma relationship goes wrong. Insys developed a painkiller originally for cancer patients in the later stages of cancer development. The product is promoted nationwide, and the company booms from profits. CNBC touted the success of the company's marketing ability. What we learn later is that the marketing team worked closely with physicians on a kickback scheme for prescribing their product. A patient would come in complaining of pain and the physician would prescribe, Subsys dosages, which were almost 100 times more powerful than morphine, containing a Fentanyl component. Patients would become addicted and many died from overdoses. Ultimately, eight executives and a few physicians are convicted. Insys agreed to pay $US 225 million in damages.

Opioids, Inc., **PBS Frontline**

https://www.pbs.org/wgbh/frontline/article/opioid-drugmaker-insys-bribing-doctors-fentanyl-painkiller/

The Frontline (PBS) link reported the story but left many important questions unanswered for the public. Why weren't all the doctors prosecuted and brought to justice who prescribed this drug for reasons other than FDA approval? There are many dangerous drugs available, but in general, doctors don't prescribe them. In this case, they were rewarded. The act of pushing a drug onto a patient with the intent of profit rather than care is no different than a drug dealer on the street. Where was the FDA and other medical regulatory agencies? What other drugs containing opioids are being pushed by physicians today? Is Insys only the tip of the iceberg?

In 2020 in the U.S., the number of deaths by suicide exceeded 45,000. We need to ask ourselves why is this happening? Why are pediatricians prescribing anti-depressants to children? Why are they prescribing Ritalin for Attention Deficit Hyperactivity Disorder? When a patient starts using any of these drugs is there an exit plan or are they on them for life? Is there a connection between these drugs and our nation's suicides, drug overdoses, and mass shootings?

Obese Man in a Motorized Cart
ParentingPatch, CC BY-SA 3.0 <https://creativecommons.org/licenses/by-sa/3.0>, via Wikimedia Commons

In Asia, it is easy to note the difference between their health and ours. They are not obese like Americans. They eat healthy food in moderation and exercise, mainly through walking. One explanation for this difference is that people take responsibility for their health. Many Americans believe doctors can fix everything and therefore we are less prone to making the effort to care for ourselves with a mindset of prevention. In most developing nations in Asia and throughout South America the people do not have this option. If they don't stay healthy, they will suffer the consequences of their behavior.

Another reason for the American obesity problem is the food we eat. The agricultural business struggles with a long supply chain from the farm to the table and the cost of food spoiling is high. Over the last 100 years, the government has funded the agricultural industry to lower the cost of our food. Fruits have been engineered for decades to have a longer shelf life. The fruits that we eat today compared to the fruits of our grandparents are completely different. When you travel to South American and Asian countries, you will be surprised by how sweet an orange or mango is compared to what we have available in the U.S. The nutritional value is not the same. Fish are farmed with diets of little protein in comparison to natural ocean or river fish. Beef, pork and poultry are injected with antibiotics. Vegetables are sprayed with herbicides and pesticides. As our food becomes less nutritious and more toxic to lower the cost of producing it, the cost to our health rises.

Most telling is the comparison to the supermarkets themselves. When you go to an American grocery store, you will most often find isles of junk food. On every corner and between the bread you will find more packages of junk food hanging. It is very different outside the U.S. In Asia it is common to only find one isle with junk food. However, I sense that this is also changing. There is great profit in selling junk food.

Wuhan Institute of Virology

The Covid-19 Pandemic further exposes the doctor Pharma relationship for profit with government intervention mixed in. Covid-19 as a deadly disease, cannot be disputed, as sadly the many deaths impacted families the world over. Covid-19 is a story from which many books will be written for decades investigating all the lies and manipulation from the politicians, AMA, Pharma, FDA, CDC, HHS, NIH and the mainstream media. Only follow the money, for there is no science. The number of questions left unanswered will reveal over time an amazing story of lies and deception by our leaders complicit with the profiteering of our medical system.

In comparison to other major health events throughout history, we are led to believe Covid-19 was going to wipe out a significant portion of the population as did the Black Death or Spanish Influenza. As of

September 2022, there have been approximately 6.5 million Covid-19 deaths worldwide. A world in which approximately seven billion people live today. By comparison, the Spanish Influenza starting in 1918 is estimated at killing approximately 50 million people worldwide. The Bubonic Plague in the mid 14th century killed 20 million or approximately one third of the population in Europe alone. The Black Death hit Europe again in the mid 1600's, killing as much as 15% of the population.

Independent journalists will need to investigate and search for truth to our nation's response to the disease as there are many unanswered questions. We need to understand the magnitude as to which pharma, physicians, government and the mainstream media are linked.

What is the motivation of their actions to lockdown, mask and vaccinate everyone? Was it truly altruistic intentions to save us all from the disease or was power and greed playing a role? As we look back, we need to carefully review what we were told, asking as many questions as possible.

Government leaders directing the narrative through the mainstream news outlets over time stir more questions about their response to Covid-19 than answers. As citizens, we should be asking for answers to at least the following:

- What was the origin of the disease? We cannot accept the Chinese Wet-Market explanation. There were many documented government programs working on Coronavirus studies in the Wuhan Lab for years prior to the Covid-19

Pandemic. Which countries funded the Wuhan Lab?

- How deadly was the disease? What age groups and health conditions were a factor in recovery?

- Were lockdowns effective? We were told at the beginning that we were going to lockdown for two weeks to "flatten the curve." Many parts of the world endured brutal lockdowns for as long as 18 months whereas other places such as Sweden and Florida had no lockdowns. The overall death tolls in these areas showed little difference, and if anything, they fared better.

- Countries implemented mandatory curfews at night. Did the virus only come out at night?

- Why did the use of ventilators stop? At the beginning of the Pandemic all the public heard about was the shortage of ventilators. We were told about the high costs of being on ventilators. How much did the hospitals profit from putting patients on them? What were the survival rates? Why over time did we stop hearing about ventilators? Most countries didn't have this equipment available. Did people die at a much higher rate in those countries?

- Masks became the rage early on. Were they effective? We know that only N95 masks were effective, but N95 masks were encouraged to not be used by the public because they were needed by the medical teams. People wore cloth masks believing that the 0.125-micron virus will not pass through a 50-micron filter of a cloth mask.

There is enough data to compare when mask mandates went into effect and the impact to show that their effectiveness needs to be questioned.

- At the onset, it was logical to ask what treatments were available. Ivermectin and hydroxychloroquine use proved effective by several doctors early on, however their promotion as a treatment was quickly suppressed. How effective were these drugs? Many parts of the world used them as a treatment with positive results. For example, in Africa, the use of Ivermectin is common for Malaria and therefore, they used it as a treatment for Covid-19. We need to better understand the outcomes. If it was effective, why was it suppressed in Western countries?

- Why weren't vitamins, such as vitamin D, promoted to boost the public's immune system?

- As Pharma rushed to bring vaccines on the market, it was explained that when we reached "herd immunity" that would be the end of the pandemic. That meant that at the time that 70 – 85% of the population would need to be vaccinated. Later, as many countries such as Canada, Iceland and Israel reached vaccination levels of over 90% they continued to suffer from Covid-19 outbreaks. We are then told that the herd immunity target needed to be 90%. The vaccines then only gave protection for six months. Booster shots are then needed to maintain protection. Why didn't the vaccines work? Why didn't we achieve herd immunity? Vaccines of the past would last a lifetime.

In the video link below, Dr. Anthony Fauci discusses the Covid-19 guidelines:

Dr. Anthony Fauci C-Span Interview

https://www.c-span.org/video/?507714-1/dr-anthony-fauci-covid-19-response-vaccine-distribution

- As the vaccines were being rushed to the market for distribution, we need to step back and ask why didn't they develop and approve a Corona virus vaccine earlier? They had been working on a vaccine for almost 20 years prior to Covid-19 and had failed to develop one that would pass the FDA approval.

- For those who had Covid-19 and survived, they would normally be classified as having "natural immunity" to the virus. For those arguing they didn't need to get the vaccine because they had natural immunity, their case was ignored. They were told that their natural immunity was not long lasting. Over time, studies were released that natural immunity was far more effective and longer lasting than vaccines. Why did the medical community ignore those with natural immunity?

- Why did the CDC change the "vaccine" definition? As we all know, vaccines have eradicated polio, measles and smallpox. Most people only receive these vaccines once in a lifetime. Did the CDC change the definition because they realized that the vaccines for Covid-19 are ineffective?

- How much money did the HHS payout to News Media outlets to advertise the Covid-19 vaccines? Through the Freedom of Information Act (FOIA), The Blaze Media discovered that hundreds of news outlets received payments to advertise, promote and suppress negative commentary on vaccine use. Those outlets included ABC, CBS, NBC, Fox News, CNN, MSNBC, New York Post, Los Angeles Times, Washington Post, BuzzFeed News, Newsmax, and hundreds of local newspapers and TV stations.

- Under the Emergency Use Authorization (EUA), the vaccines from Johnson and Johnson, Moderna and Pfizer all become authorized.

EUA excerpt as stated by the FDA,

"Under section 564 of the Federal Food, Drug, and Cosmetic Act (FD&C Act), when the Secretary of HHS declares that an emergency use authorization is

appropriate, FDA may authorize unapproved medical products or unapproved uses of approved medical products to be used in an emergency to diagnose, treat, or prevent serious or life-threatening diseases or conditions caused by CBRN threat agents when certain criteria are met, including there are no adequate, approved, and available alternatives. "

Under the EUA these companies cannot be sued for any damages or harm caused by the vaccines. They are protected from any liability.

In August 2021, the FDA announces the approval of the Pfizer vaccine under the name "Comirnaty." What this means is that if this vaccine if administered and causes harm, it will not fall under the legal protection of the EUA. At the same time as this announcement, the FDA allows the continued use of the BioNTech vaccine, the Pfizer product authorized under the EUA. To this day, the Comirnaty vaccine is not available to the public. The public is led to believe the Pfizer vaccine they are receiving is the FDA approved version. Why was this not communicated clearly to the public? Why, more than a year after FDA approval, are they not using FDA approved vaccines?

Is there such a great risk of the vaccines harming people that these Pharma companies are reluctant to take that liability? Shouldn't the public be aware of these risks? How safe are these vaccines? Is the entire population of the world facing an unknown health risk? People are concerned about the rate of those dying from myocarditis or heart damage. Are these concerns real? Will people's immune systems be compromised leading to increased risks of cancer or other diseases? What is the risk to fertility?

In addition, the EUA, as stated above, allows for these vaccines only in the case that there is no other treatment available. Hence, possibly answering the question as to why Ivermectin and Hydroxychloroquine use as a treatment is suppressed in the US.

Sadly, the answers to all these questions will most likely reveal a strong link to power and money. We are told to follow the science, but to follow the money you will most likely have your answer. Robert F. Kennedy Jr. documents in his book and movie, *The Real Anthony Fauci*, the corrupt workings government, the media and Pharma. The abuse of power by our politicians and the profiteering from the mainstream media, Pharma and the medical community will tell a story of a great lie and possibly the greatest crime ever against humanity.

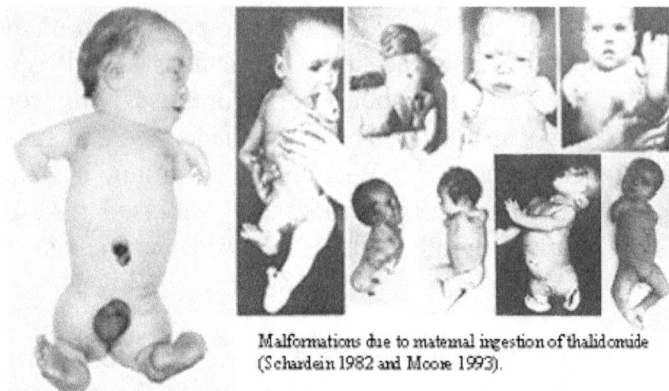

Malformations due to maternal ingestion of thalidomide (Schardein 1982 and Moore 1993).

Thalidomide Effects
Public domain, via Wikimedia Commons

In case that you are left with any doubt that Pharma will choose to profit over the population's health risk, we only need to remind ourselves of the Thalidomide scandal. In the late 1950's and early 1960's the drug was brought to market being prescribed to pregnant women to alleviate the suffering of morning sickness. After a decade of use, estimates of almost 20,000 cases worldwide linked the drug to severe birth defects. They found that there was little testing done by the pharmaceutical manufacturer on the impact to pregnancies. Imagine the risk today whereby we are administering billions of doses of an experimental vaccine to the world's population with little testing.

Climate Change

We are told climate change is due to human Carbon Dioxide (CO2) emissions. Burning fossil fuels to maintain our standard of living on the planet is releasing CO2 at a level that is causing our planet to overheat. Record summer heat waves, draughts, more aggressive storm patterns such as cyclones and hurricanes, forest fires, melting of the polar ice caps, rising sea levels, coastal flooding, are all the consequences of our human behavior. Is human activity really the cause?

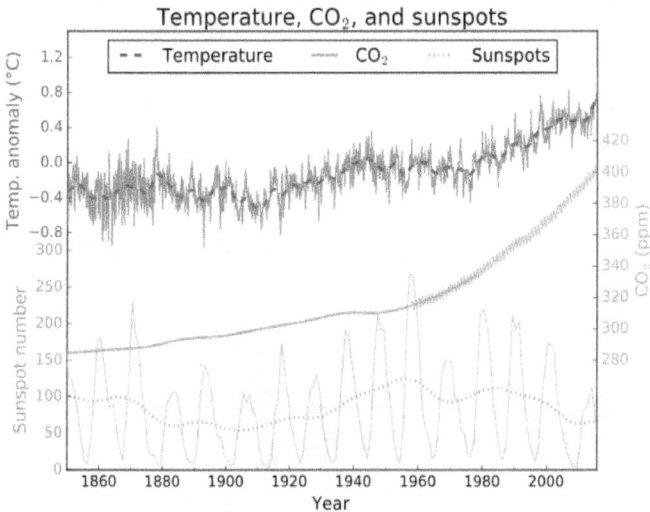

Adrien F. Vincent, CC BY-SA 4.0 <https://creativecommons.org/licenses/by-sa/4.0>, via Wikimedia Commons

Most scientists completely agree that global warming is a true phenomenon, but many conclude that the cause is not due to C02, but rather due to the current phase of a sunspot cycle. More sunspots correlates with warmer weather. They argue that man's impact on global temperatures is negligible. The earth experienced a similar phase approximately 130 years ago, and also, at that time, there were many of the same weather patterns we are experiencing today. Which Scientists are correct?

In the link below, the documentary, The Great Global Warming Swindle, discusses this argument from a different perspective. These scientists argue that historically on our planet CO_2 was never a driver of climate change, but rather a result of it. As you may note in the above graph, from 1940 to 1975 the earth was cooling, but the CO_2 level was rising. In fact, this cooling sparked a concern in the 1970's that our planet was facing a mini-ice age. Also, of note, our planet's temperature has risen only 0.5 degree over the last 100 years, but most of this rise was before 1940, a time before most of the world was industrialized.

The Great Global Warming Swindle

https://www.youtube.com/watch?app=desktop&v=oYh CQv5tNsQ

The first step in understanding man's impact on CO_2 emissions is realizing that only 0.04% of the Earth's atmosphere contains CO2. Also we must realize that the CO2 levels have changed over time, long before industrialization. Scientists have measured these levels throughout history by pulling ice core samples. It is clear that there are rises and falls far greater than what we are experiencing now. What they have learned is that the C02 levels do correlate with global warming only in that they follow the warming trend. As the earth goes through a warming phase, a rise in C02 follows. This data concludes that the Earth's rise in temperature is not due to man's C02 emissions. The CO2 narrative is another lie.

C02 levels are mostly determined by oceans emitting or absorbing C02, volcanoes, dying vegetation, and animals and bacteria. None of these processes can be controlled by man. In fact, man's contribution to C02 levels is a very insignificant percentage of the 0.04% atmospheric makeup.

"It is difficult to get a man to understand something when his salary depends upon his not understanding it." ~**Upton Sinclair**

The thousands of scientists that promote the idea that man is the root of the problem find themselves in a conflict of interest, as their future salaries and budgets are funded by those who stand to profit from the outcome. University scientists know that approval for future funding depends on their results supporting global warming. Those that produce results contrary to the narrative face being ostracized. The propaganda machine is in effect. The narrative is carried by the mainstream media, universities and in elementary schools. School children at an early age are taught the evils of fossil fuels.

As politicians explain the evils of CO2, which is a needed gas on our planet, they flash trillion-dollar budgets offering solutions of which are only a fraction of what the real cost will be. They offer solutions that would never be economically feasible in a free-market world. These politicians are closely linked to an industry profiting from the agenda.

The solution we are told by our leaders is renewable energy such as solar and wind power generation and to replace gasoline engines with electric battery powered engines. States and European countries have begun to heavily regulate fossil fuel power generation as they are now considered to be evil. The oil and gas industries are further regulated and limited in their exploration permits. Will these solutions work, and will they have an impact on C02 generation? If so, at what cost?

Wind power renewable energy seems to be a clean solution; however, the industry cannot survive without government funding. The real cost of installation and maintenance prohibits profitability. Turbine blades often need replacement or repair. Wind does not always blow and harsh weather limits power output.

Solar energy also cannot survive without government rebate programs. Installation costs are high and just as with wind, the sun does not always shine. Expensive, caustic, and environmentally unfriendly battery systems are needed. As with wind, solar is limited and can only produce a small fraction of what our modern society needs.

Electric vehicles, (EV's), offer a slick solution to counter the gas guzzling combustion engines of old. They are sold under marketing gimmicks saying that they consume half the energy (gas) cost of an equivalent combustion engine vehicle. The customer is told that these cars have far fewer parts. If they have far fewer parts, why is their cost almost double?

The battery becomes the challenge that destroys the economic model of the electric car. The batteries limit the range of the vehicles, take hours and hours to recharge, need to be replaced within eight to ten years, and most importantly need to be charged with electricity of which most likely will need to come from fossil fuels. They are produced from materials such as cobalt and lithium, which are mined in countries with highly corrupt governments. These materials cannot be easily recycled resulting in significant damage to our planet due to continued mining. The current U.S. electric grid does not have the capacity to deliver the power needed for homes with chargers. Most homes do not even have electrical amp panels with the capacity needed to charge these vehicles. All of this is ignored in the marketing of these vehicles.

Those that can afford the high cost of the electric cars are not worried about the replacement battery cost or that the cobalt mining is destroying our planet in another part of the world that they cannot see. Owners will never achieve the expected savings over the cost of a combustion engine vehicle. Their electric car ownership becomes a status symbol. Their electric car ownership has become a form of virtue signaling of the elitist. Buying an EV would be better understood as a case of "more money than brains."

The trillions of dollars needed to upgrade the electrical grid, to subsidize rebates and build charging stations nationwide will unfortunately come from working taxpayers too poor to afford one of the vehicles. Politicians understand that they stand to profit immensely from kickbacks and further gains of voter support. They will push fossil fuel regulations destroying oil, gas and combustion engine vehicles, leaving the population forced to limit their mobility.

To follow these politicians' solutions of fossil fuel industry destruction, expensive renewable energy and forced conversion to electric vehicles, will only lead to the impoverishment of society. Those countries that lead by this narrative will find themselves with a reduced standard of living facing risk of no heat during the winter, darkness at night and limited transportation. As their food supply depends heavily on diesel fuel, they will ultimately suffer with little food to eat.

Bonus Food for Thought:

We were told the following:

In the 1960s we reached peak oil, and we would run out of oil in ten years.

In the 1970s the earth was cooling over the last several decades, and we would face a mini-ice age in the next ten years.

In the 1980s due to greenhouse gas emissions, acid rain was going to destroy our crops and lakes in the next ten years.

In the 1990s, due to the use of fluorocarbons, the ozone layer would be destroyed in the next ten years.

In the 2000s spurred on from Al Gore's book and movie, *An Inconvenient Truth*, the polar ice caps were going to melt in the next ten years.

In 2010s the ice caps melting would cause coastal flooding wiping out major cities all throughout the world over the next 10 years!

None of these events ever happened.

Could there be a pattern here?

Bonus Food for Thought:

Current nuclear fission reactors use Uranium-235, of which it is costly to mine and enrich. We face a long-term supply challenge. The reactors themselves operating under high vapor pressure, risk leaks and release of radiation. The waste remains dangerous for hundreds of thousands of years.

There has always been an alternative, a Thorium-232 molten salt reactor. As a material, it is readily available as a by-product of current mining. There is enough supply available to power the planet for thousands of years. The reactors are safer running at low pressure and in the case of emergency can be powered down easily. The power plants produce electricity more efficiently and the construction size is smaller and therefore less costly to build. They also produce far less waste, of which it is less dangerous.

With all of these advantages, why are we not using Thorium today? At the time of the development of the nuclear power industry, the government promoted the use of Uranium-235 over Thorium-232 due to its by-product Plutonium-239. They needed nuclear weapons-grade material to feed their nuclear arsenal buildup. For this reason, Thorium has been ignored. Interestingly, even the inventor of today's high-pressure water reactor, Alvin Weinberg, in 1947 understood the molten salt reactor to be a much better option.

Today due to U.S. government regulations and public fear, rightly so, due to the dangers of Uranium reactors, it is impossible to construct Thorium reactors in the U.S. Therefore, China and India are taking the lead.

Bonus Food for Thought:

During the period of the Renaissance in 1543, the astronomer, Nicholas Copernicus, found that the models used to explain celestial movements all revolving around Earth were not logical. He realized that the movements were better explained by stating that the Earth and planets revolved around the Sun.

Shortly after, Galileo Galilei through the use of a telescope found that Copernicus' ideas were right. In reality the Earth did rotate around the Sun. His ideas, as Copernicus', were not accepted by the Catholic Church. The Church taught that man was at the center of God's created universe. Copernicus and Galileo's ideas and books were banned.

The scientists today challenging climate change politicians are in many ways in a similar situation as were Copernicus and Galileo with the Catholic Church. Fortunately, at the time Copernicus and Galileo's explanation had relatively little impact on man. Either way, it made little difference to man's wellbeing. The impact on the correct understanding of climate change will have major consequences. Government funding needed to support the electrification of vehicles will risk impoverishing nations for generations. Elimination of fossil fuels will lower the standard of living of our civilization as well as put at risk our food supply.

Bonus Food for Thought:

Most of us have forgotten high school chemistry where we learned that when water freezes into ice, it is the one material that expands rather than contracts when going through this phase change. The fact that water volume increases is why ice floats and rises to the top of rivers, lakes and oceans. If it sank to the bottom like other materials when freezing, fish below would all die in the winter. In reverse when ice melts, its volume decreases. When the North pole ice cap melts, ocean levels in theory should go down. The opposite of what we are being told.

Also note, the renowned scientist Carl Sagan tried to argue in the 1980's that when the Antarctic ice shelf collapses into the ocean it will raise the sea level, ultimately flooding all coastal regions. So far, this hasn't happened either.

Education

> *"The effect of progressive education is to destroy independent thought in the child, indeed, to repress any thought whatsoever. Instead, the children learn to revere certain heroic symbols, or to follow the domination of the "group." Thus, subjects are taught as little as possible, and the child has little chance to develop any systematic reasoning powers in the study of definite courses. This program is being carried forward into high school, as well as grammar school, so that many high-school graduates are ignorant of elementary spelling or reading and cannot write a cogent sentence."* ~**Murray N. Rothbard, "Education: Free & Compulsory", 1971, p53**

In my journey overseas, my wife and I faced the challenge as to how best to educate our two children. We feared that in a third world country they would miss out on a valuable American form of education. We noticed that all foreigners like us would send their children to "American" schools. These schools were very expensive but taught in English and the environment was clean and organized.

It was also apparent in these countries that there was a booming business of private schools. These private schools were at all levels of affordability. The people knew that the public-school system was broken, and the free-market was solving the problem by offering options for the parents. The parents would drop off their kids satisfied they were getting the best education available that they could afford.

As we were told the public schools in these countries were not acceptable, I began to wonder why? It was explained to us that our children would not learn much in that environment. This challenge really forced us to rethink and ask the question what is a good education? Why are the public schools in these countries failing to give the people the education they need? Over time I began to question if we have the same problem with our own U.S. public school system?

Children's minds are easy to impress ideas upon. As Murray Rothbard captures in his book, "Education: Free & Compulsory," teachers need to teach the class to the lowest common denominator, the slow kid. From the ages of nine to thirteen, after four years of being bored waiting for the slow kid, they become the slow kids as well.

All totalitarian regimes throughout history have recognized the importance of the State owning the educational system, from Hitler's Youth camps to the Imperial Japanese. Indoctrination at an early age is critical to maintaining loyalty to the State.

The Spartans understood the importance of having a population loyal to the State. They ensured this by taking children from their parents at an early age to prepare for a life in the military. Similarly, today military recruiters occupy school guidance counselors' offices, preying on weaker students that don't have a plan in life. School counselors are incentivized to herd students into these programs.

One amazing example today of a fully implemented well organized State school system is China's educational system. It is a system fully controlled by the State at all levels. The outcome, they produce hundreds of thousands of engineers, however, there is little innovation. Try to think of any product today invented in China. The innovation comes from the Western countries. China is only famous for copying and reproducing the West's technology. China's educational system is a perfect example of a model reflecting Rothbard's quote above.

When President Dwight D. Eisenhower was elected, Nelson Rockefeller could have taken any office in the cabinet due to his support during the election. He made the point of selecting the Secretary of Education. He knew that from that position he would have the greatest influence on our future generations. His grandfather is quoted as saying,

"I don't want a nation of thinkers; I want a nation of workers." ~**John D. Rockefeller**

When you send your child off to public school today, they are at risk of being taught by trained Marxists who will teach your child to be obedient to the State. Religion and family are not important. Teaching finance and needed life skills are not important. The teaching of the meaning of our Founding Father's documents including the Constitution is weak or incorrect. You can always test this argument by just asking a high school student a simple question regarding the Bill of Rights.

Today, even the private schools don't have it right. They are also part of the progressive movement. They pedal the progressive "Woke" and Critical Race Theories (CRT) just as in the Socialist Public Schools. They are no different than the public schools because the teachers all study and graduate from the same Socialist Universities. The wealthy parents pay the high tuition thinking their children are getting a better education. They dump their kids off at a fancy school and go off to their busy careers. The private schools are filled with rich spoiled children influenced by a culture of socialism, drugs and alcohol.

This culture in the private schools was very evident in the third world countries. In these countries most of the population didn't use drugs. In fact, it was almost non-existent with the poor. They did drink too much alcohol, but drug addiction did not exist. However, where it did exist was in the expensive private schools. There, the students with their parent's money, drug use was prevalent. We have the same issue in the US.

*".. Already long ago, from when we sold our vote to no man, the People have abdicated our duties; for the People who once upon a time handed out military command, high civil office, legions — everything, now restrains itself and anxiously hopes for just two things: **bread and circuses**."*
~Juvenal, Satire 10.77–81

Another lie our educational system promotes is the value of High School Sports. The students chase a dream to one day become professional players. The dream to be the heroes in the "circuses" mentioned in the quote above. What they fail to realize is that the statistical chance of becoming the pro-player is one in a million. Those that don't make it to college ball become prime candidates for military recruitment. If they do go on and graduate from college and have the opportunity to go pro, they will most likely have a short career before they are bumped off the team due to injuries or age. They end up being lost in life, often suffering lifelong injuries, with little education on the skills needed to be successful in life.

As Robert Kiyosaki writes in his book *"Why "A" Students work for "C" Students and "B" Students work for the government"*, 2013, p109:

> *"The world of the future belongs to those who can embrace change, see the future and anticipate its needs, and respond to new opportunities and challenges with creativity and agility and passion."*

Do you believe that our educational system prepares our younger generations as such? After we, the people, spend fortunes on taxes for school budgets, do you believe they return the value or are they wasted on an institutional agenda?

> *"No public school in the United States is set up to allow a George Washington to happen. Washingtons in the bud stage are screened, browbeaten, or bribed to conform to a narrow outlook on social truth. Boys like Andrew Carnegie who begged his mother not to send him to school and was well on his way to immortality and fortune at the age of thirteen, would be referred today for psychological counseling; Thomas Edison would find himself in Special Ed until his peculiar genius had been sufficiently tamed."* ~**John Taylor Gatto, "The Underground History of American Education", 2017, p90**

Higher Education: Setting the Student Debt Trap

"In order to succeed in business, a man does not need a degree from a school of business administration. These schools train the subalterns for routine jobs. They certainly do not train entrepreneurs. An entrepreneur cannot be trained. A man becomes an entrepreneur by seizing an opportunity and filling the gap. No special education is required for such a display of keen judgment, foresight, and energy." **~Ludwig von Mises, *Human Action***

In the past, by the time you graduated from high school, you were trained for what you needed in life. Today many children graduate without being able to read or write. All the students are pushed to go into college. But College is not for everybody. Students don't access the risk versus value. They sign up for a lifetime of debt, consuming the most productive years of their lives.

As many college institutions were being founded in the early 1800's, the costs were affordable. For example, an Ivy League University's annual tuition from Harvard or Columbia was in the range of $50 – $75 per year. The tuition costs more or less remained the same until the early 1900's, rising slowly until the end of WWII. Culturally, College was also not perceived as necessary for everyone to have a successful career. If they chose this path, it was very common even up into the 1970's, for students to work hard at a part time or summer job to pay for their annual college costs.

By 1947, Ivy League annual tuition costs rose to about $500, however, shortly thereafter, the rate of tuition increases began to accelerate, and the culture of higher education began to change. After WWII, the GI Bill was passed, which kicked off a major shift in how education was paid for. The benefits offered a path to higher education paid for by the federal government. The number of students enrolling in colleges increased dramatically. Colleges seized the opportunity to further raise tuition, knowing that the costs were being funded. By 1975, an Ivy League tuition rose to about $5,000.

In 1965, the federal government also began guaranteeing student loans. The intent of the program began with the idea as to why work so hard during the summer to pay for your education because after you graduate you can easily pay off the loan. The need for the loans to be guaranteed by the federal government was required as no bank would be willing to make a loan to a student without some form of debt guarantee. Loaning money to students prior to this program was not a good business as we all know a student has no collateral. However, for the program to pass, congress required that the loans could not be forgiven. The student loan trap was set.

Colleges understood that students would have access to more money to fund their tuition. They quickly began to increase their tuition rates. By 2020, the cost of tuition and room and board at an Ivy League school has risen to $70,000 per year. Costs at all colleges across the nation rose in a similar way. Today the average private college tuition, room and board amounts to $50,000 per year. Students today expect to graduate with a four-year degree from a private institution with over $100,000 of student debt. If they choose to continue for another two years to complete an MBA program, they will tack on more debt.

The students graduate and enter a job market where they are often unable to find a position that will cover their living expenses. In a weak job market, they may struggle in a low wage position as well as remain unemployed for periods of time. The interest on the debt compounds even if they are not working. In many cases, as they cannot declare bankruptcy, they carry this debt for the next 20 to 30 years, with the amount owed increasing year over year.

Peter Schiff asks, "Is a college degree worth the cost?"

https://www.youtube.com/watch?v=fkWui7H3zPM

Money - The Greatest Lie and the "Root of All Evil"

"We can only measure the wealth of a nation by its poorest citizen."

Government can only earn money three ways: borrow from creditors, tax citizens or companies, or print it. The first two are fairly straight forward. They are visible and easy to measure. People understand when taxes are too high. Throughout most of history, taxes were in the range of 10-12%. Any higher and the politicians knew the risk of a rebellion. The last option, to print, is more seductive. It is referred to as the "inflation tax."

Murray Rothbard in *Mystery of Banking*, 2008, p177 explains how our current central banking system started. In the 17th century, after decades of the English war with France, the country had run out of funding to support the wars. They knew that increasing taxes directly risked revolt from the common people. William Paterson with his crooked cronies presented to the House of Commons and King William a solution whereby a Bank of England would be established. The new Bank would enable the printing of bank notes that would fund the government's wars. One of the first Central Banks was born!

They knew that the common people would not be able to detect the increase in the money supply. They would experience price increases in goods and services, which is more difficult to link back to the root cause, "inflation" of the money supply.

When the government introduces new money into circulation, they use it first. They benefit first. As the money begins to enter the mix, overall, there is more money in circulation. People have more money, but they didn't produce more goods. People will be willing to spend more for the same goods. The unintended consequence of printing money is prices going up. This is a key distinction in the Austrian definition of "inflation" versus our modern-day definition.

Today inflation is defined to be an increase in prices of goods or services. The government doesn't want the people to understand that the true definition is the increase in money supply which will result in the increase in prices. The real culprit is hidden, just as William Paterson and King William were when they came up with the scheme for the Bank of England. Today our Federal Reserve Banking system acts in the same manner as the Bank of England did at its founding. Even the lies being told to the public to print money to fund wars are not much different now as they were then.

In Third World countries inflation is easy to understand. The people in these countries see the corruption whereby the leaders enrich themselves at the citizens' expense. In most of these countries the people know that the paper currency is always devaluing as their government prints money. Prices are not going up; the value of their money is going down. They know that holding paper money is not a store of value. They are quick to move their savings into real-estate or US dollars of which they believe is more stable.

Americans, not schooled in finance, say that printing money doesn't affect the dollar. No American alive today has lived through a currency collapse, as happens in most Third World countries. However, throughout history all empires fall ultimately from weakening the value of their money. Those that don't financially collapse remain impoverished from the inflation tax.

Revisiting the history of currency failures:

In the late 1700's, France's last King and Queen, Louis XVI and Marie Antoinette squandered the nation's money supporting America's war against the British. By the end of the war, France was financially ruined from printing currency. Ultimately, the King and Queen lost their heads in the guillotine. The New National Assembly began to issue a new French bond called the Assignat. Again, the paper note is devalued quickly leading to hyperinflation and food riots, and the fall of the First French Republic.

The German Weimar Republic (1918-1933) established at the end of World War I began in its first years a policy of printing money to pay war debts and to rebuild the economy. At first the plan appeared to be working. However, the Reichbank suspended its $1/3^{rd}$ gold reserves requirement allowing the government to print beyond their limits. Quickly the acceleration of the currency devaluation into 1922 and 1923 caused economic collapse and hyperinflation. The currency was reset and appeared to recover with an economic boom until the Great Depression struck. The socialist boom collapsed, ending in economic disaster and ultimately allowing Adolf Hitler to seize power.

It was said "the sun never sets on British Empire." For several hundred years, the Empire had control over large parts of the world reaching its peak from the early 1800s to the start of World War I in 1914. In the decade following the war, they quickly lost all their power. The cost of war eroded Britain's wealth forcing it to abandon control. For the people, they experienced a rapid decline in the value of the British pound as their government debt exploded. Politicians did not want to stop spending and by 1931 Britain is forced off the gold standard, only hastening the pound's decline.

The collapse of the U.S.S.R. was a result of a collapse in the currency. Decades of a centrally planned socialist economy, whereas the means of production was owned by the State, resulted in impoverishment of the people. Shortages of everything needed to survive existed everywhere. People were fed up with the failed system. Keep in mind the Berlin Wall was built to keep the people from fleeing socialism. By 1991 after the deaths of 10s of millions of citizens, fighting a hopeless war in Afghanistan, impoverishment and a collapsed currency, the 75-year experiment in socialism of the Soviet Empire came to an end.

Over the last 30 years, we have had many examples of modern-day currency collapses. Argentina, Mexico, the Dominican Republic and Venezuela all experienced massive devaluations of their currencies due to their governments spending beyond their means. In all cases, the populations holding the currency lost everything.

Their money became worthless. The irony is that many of those trying to protect themselves from losing their wealth moved their money into U.S. dollars, unaware of the risk.

The ultimate example of money printing to prop up a corrupt government is Zimbabwe. Over decades of Robert Mugabe's regime, they printed money to the extreme. They needed to print $100 Trillion dollars bills as the country escalated into hyperinflation. As Peter Schiff once commented, Zimbabwe would be the "richest nation in the world if printing money created wealth."

Do we manage our money any differently in the U.S.? Since the founding of our Federal Reserve Bank in 1913, our U.S. dollar has lost 98% of its purchasing power. Our national debt today stands at over $30 Trillion. We have an additional $170 trillion in unfunded liabilities.

As we look at history, we can draw many parallels to the failed governments of the past. We have spent twenty years fighting a losing war in Afghanistan. Both the British Empire and the U.S.S.R. fought endlessly in that country only resulting in their collapse.

In all cases, those in power ignored the basic principles of Austrian economics. Printing money out of thin air is inflation. They "inflate" the money supply. The result is that as there is more money in circulation, the value of the money decreases.

To put it another way, a government just running off paper dollars, does not create wealth. In fact, it destroys the value of the dollars already in existence. Unfortunately, those in power can never curb their greed. When tied to maintaining their political agenda to keep their voters, the system becomes self-destructive. Simply put, politicians need to lie.

A fun site to better understand how fast our U.S. government is spending money real time is at the USdebtclock.org.

The US Debt Clock

https://www.usdebtclock.org/

The politicians loot the country keeping the people unaware to maintain the ultimate lie. Nothing is second to government wasteful spending. They are no different than the mindset of a thief, King William or William Paterson.

Unfortunately, our government, as well as all governments around the world, have control over the supply of money. This "power" is the root of all the needed lies. A thief never wants to be known as a thief. The citizens, believing the good intentions of all the government social programs to help them in return, are mostly unaware that the politicians are spending to buy their votes and maintain their power.

They tout metrics which communicate the state of the economy: Consumer Price Index (CPI), Percent Unemployment, and Gross Domestic Product (GDP). Other metrics useful in understanding the state of an economy such as national debt, unfunded liabilities, and trade deficits are ignored today because those numbers spell a dismal economic mess.

Metrics such as the CPI are all manipulated over time to drift toward a favorable outcome for politicians. They know that if prices start to go up too fast, the people will become angry as their cost-of-living increases faster than their income. The formula for CPI uses three components: homeowners equivalent rent, substitution and other adjustments to manipulate the rate lower. The CPI formula itself is not the same as it was during the 1970's hiding the real increase in the cost of living.

Even the decades-long, long-standing definition of "Recession" that has been used by all countries changes in 2022. A "Recession" has traditionally been defined as two consecutive quarters of negative GDP growth. Our President, Joe Biden, going into a critical mid-term election, reluctant to reveal to citizens that we have been in a recession for the first half of the year, convinces the Americans now the definition is different, despite the fact that we had two consecutive quarters of negative GDP growth. We are told by our political leaders that we are not in recession.

Americans are told by the Federal Reserve Chairman, Jerome Powell, that they have a 2% annual inflation target. As inflation rages over 8% in 2021 after years of money printing, we are told that inflation is "transitory" implying it will return to the 2%. Another lie, as in the following year inflation continues to rise to 9.2%. Of course, he needs to keep the lie ongoing to hide the effects of money printing.

The world has confidence in our dollar. We are the world's currency. Our dollar is strong. Americans have never lived through a collapsing currency. We are told by our leaders not to worry. However, in reality we are at great risk. Our creditor nations are not our friends. Confidence is fragile and once broken, cannot easily be regained.   No country in history has escaped massive debt levels such as ours without a painful financial collapse impoverishing the nation and its citizens.

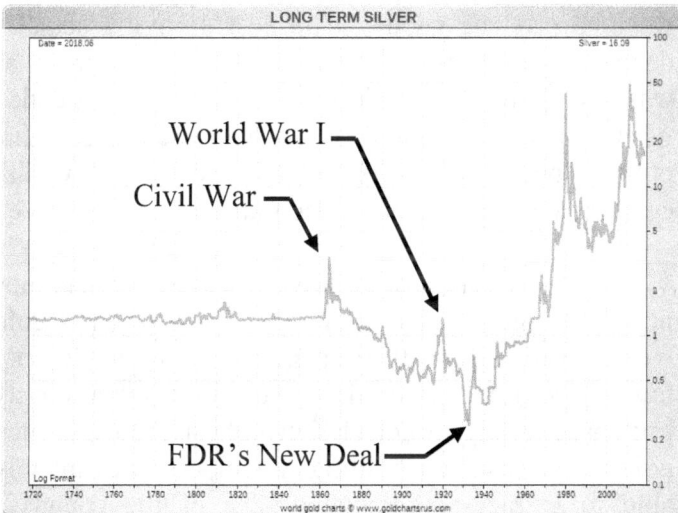

Graph of Silver Price in US Dollars
(Courtesy of World Gold Charts at www.goldchartsrus.com)

The above graph charts the relation of the number of US dollars it takes to purchase an ounce of silver from prior to our country's founding to today. In other words, the value of our currency. Silver is a good metal to use in comparison to the value of the US dollar as it has been used as a form of money for thousands of years around the world. Note that at the time of war, as the government prints money, the value of the dollar declines.

Also note that after the Civil War, the value of the dollar increased (a declining curve), until the beginning of Franklin D. Roosevelt's Presidency. There was a decrease in value again during the time period of World War I but continued after the war to strengthen until the 1930s. During this period of time our nation industrialized, and through free market capitalism and innovation, manufacturers found better and cheaper ways to produce goods. The cost of living actually declined. Americans became wealthier as their dollar was strong and they could purchase more. That ended when President Franklin D. Roosevelt's socialist policies began to destroy all the progress of wealth creation and we have had a declining dollar ever since.

Historically, gold was a key part of sound money policy. Countries that backed their currency with gold were forced to limit their spending. They could only buy the gold mined and that would limit them to only print paper money in correlation to the amount of mined gold. This was a self-limiting system, as mines are only able to extract approximately 2% of the country's current supply per year. In turn, this would force the government to limit their expansion of the money supply to no more than 2%. A great system, but over time discarded as government leaders could not resist the temptation to print money.

The U.S. went on the gold standard in the Bretton Woods agreement in 1944. However, as President Lyndon B. Johnson rolled out his socialist programs of the "Great Society" and escalated the war in Vietnam, foreign countries began to become suspicious that we were not honoring the agreement. In 1971, Charles de Gaulle sent a battleship to the New York harbor to exchange all of his US dollars for gold. At that time, countries were free to exchange $US 35 for one gold ounce or vice versa.

We honored France's request; however, President Nixon knew if other foreign countries wanted to do the same, we would default. We didn't have the gold to cover the amount of printed money. He closed the gold window immediately in response, taking the U.S. off the gold standard causing the US to default on our obligations.

Robert Kiyosaki's book *Rich Dad Poor Dad* series and podcast does a nice job of teaching money and finance. He explains the value of gold, money and the lies from our politicians. As they don't teach Americans about money in school, we need to make this effort ourselves.

Taxes

> *"How much of your money should be spent by the State? The State has no source of money other than the money the people earn themselves. There is no such thing as public money, only taxpayer money. No nation has ever grown more prosperous by taxing its citizens beyond their capacity to pay."* ~**Margaret Thatcher**

Prior to 1913, Americans did not have a Federal Income tax. Income for the Federal government was normally earned through tariffs. The 16th Amendment was proposed and pushed through for ratification by the Progressive party with the intention of eliminating tariffs and only taxing the wealthier Americans. In addition, the tax would only be a small percentage. The Americans did not realize in passing this Amendment, the amount of government spending they would unleash.

Today we pay Federal, State, sales, and real-estate taxes totaling in the range of the average working persons income of 50%. We work more than 6 months a year for the State or half of our life. This is far more than what the American colonists were fighting for at the time of the American Revolution. Far more than what the kings of Europe taxed their serfs.

> *"It is difficult to free fools from the chains they revere."* ~**Voltaire**

Americans pay their taxes without protest. By design, they are due in April, six months from November, when they vote. By the time the election rolls around, they've forgotten their tax payments.

Knowing little about what their politicians are spending, they continue to re-elect their leaders hoping that things will improve.

Socialism in America

At the core of the lies spread today in the U.S. exists the ideologies of Socialism. The lies are needed to protect those in power from the common people revolting if they knew the truth. They need to keep the people hypnotized. Over more than a century, elementary school teachers, University professors and Hollywood film writers all peddled socialist propaganda indoctrinating the population. We reach a point whereby more than 51% of the voting population receives government entitlements in some form. Big government programs passed by congress are supported by the majority all starting with good intentions. They never see the unintended consequences. The system becomes unstoppable.

Early in the 20th century, the socialist movement was led by the Marxist Institute. The name was not popular and was later changed to the Frankfurt School. Throughout the last century the movement focused on building a party base through strong labor unions. Better working conditions for labor was the core message of their activism. By the end of the 20th century they realized unions were losing strength and they needed a different strategy to gain support.

Their agenda pivoted to focus on the "white man" as the oppressor throughout history through which by definition, everyone else is a victim. Minorities, women, and LGBTQ persons are said to be all oppressed by the evil white man. They push the ideas of Critical Race Theory (CRT) destroying the nuclear family. The state becomes hijacked by their ideas as the socialist leaders gain power. Socialist politicians gain voters support as voters fail to understand the dangers of a powerful government and high deficit spending funding their programs. As inflation creeps in, the people become impoverished.

Our Constitutional rights are ignored as those opposed must either remain silent or risk being labeled domestic terrorists. The FBI becomes the strong arm of the government's power suppressing free speech on media platforms such as Facebook. Free journalism is restricted as those such as Julian Assange become enemies of the State. Gun ownership restrictions become the politicians agenda silently intended to weaken any threat to the State. As the U.S. national debt level races past $30 trillion, quickly the citizens continue to lose their voice and power. They become impoverished, silenced, and left with no recourse except to embrace their dependency on the State.

To the Future

"It is always the anvil that breaks the hammer, never the other way about." ~**George Orwell**

Orwell's quote above, gives us hope that one day as citizens, the evil "hammer" of government will collapse, freeing us from its oppressive force.

George Orwell tried to warn us in his book, "1984" of the power of a strong socialist state. Unfortunately, the book today is being used as a handbook for our leaders to impress socialism upon us. How long do we allow those in power, lying to us, keep their credibility? What are our options as citizens?

"I am convinced that those societies (as the Indians) which live without government enjoy in their general mass an infinitely greater degree of happiness than those who live under European governments." ~**Thomas Jefferson**

As parents, homeschooling provides a better education. Parents need to be directly involved with their children's education at all levels. Don't depend on anyone to do that work for you. It is easier and the results are far better than you will be able to imagine. The Ron Paul Home School curriculum offers a great path.

As citizens, be independent entrepreneurs. We are still a capitalist free-market country. Find needs in our society and bring solutions. Own your own business. Don't work for one.

Learn languages and other cultures. Study economics and history. Travel and be prepared to relocate to another state or country less oppressive. **Vote with your feet!**

Educate yourself and your family on the dangers and risks of socialist ideologies such as "Woke" and Critical Race Theory. Beware anytime the government is handing out benefits. Vote "No" to all government spending. The State's cradle to grave list of socialist handouts will destroy you. Bolster your family. Strengthen your religion. You are not trapped or alone. You must learn to be independent of the State.

Don't be afraid of critical thinking, asking difficult questions, applying logic and using your own gut instinct when you believe something is not right. And most importantly,

"Believe nothing you hear, and only one half that you see." ~**Edgar Allen Poe**

It's All a Lie!

The Fight for Liberty:

Fortunately today there are many great leaders fighting for the freedoms defined by our Founding Fathers. They work to expose the lies and present a true reality. Here are a few in the fight against government oppression:

Ron Paul, RonPaulLibertyReport.com

Mises institute, Mises.org

Tom Woods, TomWoods.com

Peter Schiff, SchiffRadio.com

Lew Rockwell, LewRockwell.com

Scott Horton, Antiwar.com

Chris Irons, QuothTheRaven.podbean.com

George Gammon, The-rebel-capitalist-show.simplecast.com

Joe Rogan, (Podcast on Spotify)

Viva Frei, (YouTube)

Candice Owens, (The Daily Wire)

Alex Jones, Infowars.com

Dinesh D'Souza, (On Locals.com)

Robert Kiyosaki, RichDad.com

Recommended Reading *(This is only a sliver of recommended reading, but they are fun places to start)*:

U.S. Constitution

Declaration of Independence

The Federalist Papers

Albert Jay Nock, *Jefferson*

Murray Rothbard,

> *America's Great Depression*
> *Anatomy of the State*
> *Education: Free and Compulsory*
> *Wall Street, Banks, and American Foreign Policy*

Ludwig Von Mises

> *Human Action*
> *Profit and Loss*

Tom Woods,

> *The Politically Incorrect Guide to American History*
> *33 Questions About American History You're Not Supposed to Ask*

Tom DiLorenzo,

> *The Politically Incorrect Guide to Economics*
> *The Problem with Socialism*

How Capitalism Saved America

Adam Fergusson, When *Money Dies*

Sean Patrick, *The Know Your Bill of Rights*

Peter Schiff, The *Real Crash*

Robert F. Kennedy Jr., *The Real Anthony Fauci*

G. Edward Griffin, *The Creature from Jekyll Island*

George B.N. Ayittey, *Defeating Dictators*

Friedrich Hayek, *The Road to Serfdom*

Recommended Starter Study List in Economics from the Mises Institute:

Anatomy of the State by Murray N. Rothbard

The Philosophical Origins of Austrian Economics by David Gordon

Praxeology and Understanding by George A. Selgin

Profit and Loss by Ludwig von Mises

I, Pencil by Leonard Read

What Has the Government Done to Our Money? by Murray N. Rothbard, pp. 1-87

From *The Austrian Theory of the Trade Cycle and Other Essays*, edited by Richard M. Ebeling:

- "Introduction: The Austrian Theory in Perspective" by Roger W. Garrison, pp. 7-35
- "Economic Depressions: Their Cause and Cure" by Murray N. Rothbard, pp. 65-91
- "Can We Still Avoid Inflation?" Friedrich A. Hayek, pp. 93-120

From *Economics in One Lesson* by Henry Hazlitt:

- "The Lesson," pp. 3-7
- "The Broken Window," pp. 11-16

From *Economic Freedom and Interventionism* by Ludwig von Mises

- "The Elite Under Capitalism"
- "The Individual in Society"

From *An Introduction to Austrian Economics* by
Thomas C. Taylor:

- "Introduction," pp. 7-21
- "The Subjective Theory of Value," pp. 40-62

From *Planning for Freedom* by Ludwig von Mises:

- "Planning for Freedom," pp. 1-17
- "Middle of the Road Policy Leads to
  Socialism," pp. 18-35

"Fundamentals of Value and Price" by Murray N.
Rothbard (in *The Rothbard Reader*, pp. 89-126)

"Economic Calculation" by Ludwig von Mises
(in *Socialism: An Economic and Sociological Analysis*,
pp. 113-122)

"The Meaning of Competition" by F. A. Hayek

www.ingramcontent.com/pod-product-compliance
Lightning Source LLC
LaVergne TN
LVHW051348080426
835509LV00020BA/3346